D0711730

Classic Minnesota
Fishing Stories

Waldman House Press
Minneapolis, Minnesota

Waldman House Press

Classic Minnesota Fishing Stories

A Rare Collection of First-Hand Accounts, Anecdotes and Reports

Joe Fellegy

Foreword by Ron Schara
Illustrations by Dennis Anderson

You may order single copies from the
Publisher. Try your bookstore first.
Enclose $8.95 plus $1.00 postage and handling.

Waldman House Press
525 North Third Street
Minneapolis, Minnesota 55401

Library of Congress Cataloging in Publication Data

Classic Minnesota fishing stories.

   1. Fishing—Minnesota.   2. Fishing stories.
I. Fellegy, Joe, 1944-
SH511.C55   799.1'1'09776   82-7061
                              AACR2

ISBN 0-931674-04-2

Designed by Dennis Anderson

Printed in the United States of America
First Printing, May 1982
Second Printing, October 1983

Foreword

Fishing is more than catching, if you've ever wondered.

It's also made up of things like sunsets and loon calls, backlashes and mosquito attacks.

But most of all, fishing is camaraderie. Good times spent with good friends in a sport that is never truly mastered by any of the participants.

Call it good fortune. For it means that all of us who wet a line pursue a common mystery. It matters not that one fisherman may cast a fly more deftly than the next. And surely luck, being what it is, isn't always evenly divided among us.

Yet, we are all equals within the confines of a fishing boat in our eternal quest to make a fish open its mouth. Because this is so, our trials and tribulations we share with one another. Our victories, our defeats, our hopes and frustrations, all are passed on wherever and whenever fishermen gather. It's a tradition.

In other words, fishermen tell lots of stories.

Fishing rods and casting reels may be our tools. Worms may be our bait. But fishing stories, those plain tales or exaggerated episodes, are the heart and spirit of the sport.

Story-telling is what fishermen do when they cannot fish. It's the next best thing to being there, whether you're doing the telling or the listening. This also explains why fishermen don't mind when other fishermen miss the truth sometimes. Truth or not, the story takes you where you'd rather be.

The magic of fishing stories is understood by fishermen. And Joe Fellegy is a fisherman. Joe was weaned on the banks of a Minnesota fishing lake, Mille Lacs, and never found a reason to leave. What he needs to survive he earns as a fishing guide. Been a guide for so many seasons, he's prematurely crusty for his age. A compliment if there ever was one.

But more than that, Joe Fellegy long has known what makes

the sport of fishing tick. Fishing stories, of course. He's heard plenty of them. And like a good steward of the angling spirit, Joe could not let them sink away like a giant walleye on a busted line.

Good fishing stories are like fine wines. To be bottled and cherished for all ages. Joe has done that. He's bottled some of Minnesota's finest fishing lore of recent vintage.

It's time now to savor them. Turn the page.

Ron Schara

Award-Winning Columnist
for the *Minneapolis Tribune*
and Author of *Ron Schara's*
Minnesota Fishing Guide

Contents

v   FOREWORD

1   INTRODUCTION

5   HARRY VAN DOREN, NISSWA GUIDE
    Harry's First Guiding Trip
    Harry's Best Season on Gull Lake
    Young Harry Jumps In and Swims Home

9   1955 LEECH LAKE MUSKIE RAMPAGE
    Garry Neururer Remembers the 1955
    Leech Lake Muskie Rampage
    Lazy Ikes and Brooks Reefers at Leech

15 CAL BACKER'S TROPHY
    The True Story of Cal Backer's Trophy Catch:
    A 212-pound Rainy Lake Guide on a Dardevle

18 AL LINDNER
    All About Landing a 44-pound Mississippi River Muskie—
    on 6-pound Test Line!
    The Lure Changer From St. Louis

25 HJALMAR SWENSON, A FISHERIES CHIEF
    Swenson Short Stories
    When Something Big Entered the Trap at Waskish

28   CHARLIE ISLE, OLD-TIMER

Spearing on Borden and Mille Lacs, 1910

Fishin' the Mississippi: "Up from Brainerd"

The Nokassippi Connection

Winter Spearing Days

36   LEROY CHIOVITTE

*17-pound 8-ounce State Record Walleye
from Sea Gull River, 1979*

45   AL MAAS, LEECH LAKE MUSKIE HUNTER

"The Biggest Muskie I Had Ever Seen"

A Muskie "Double"

48   JAKE CLINE, HACKENSACK MEMORIES

*"It Paid to Stay Later":
Stony Lake Walleyes and Pleasant Lake Crappies*

Birch Lake Walleyes at Ten Before Seven

The Car Spring Trick

52   HANK KEHBORN, GONE FISHING

Stroking a Muskie's Belly

*Hank and Ed Shave Portage In:
Yanking on Ed's New Outboard*

Charlie Lembke's Secret Bass Lake

57   HARLOW ELLSWORTH, HAWG HUNTER

*Lunker Largemouth Bass:
A Trail of Broken Rods*

60   ED MOREY, FISH PEDDLER FROM MOTLEY

*The Morey Fish Company:
A History by Ed Morey Himself*

Ed Morey's Short Stories

67 STORIES FROM VETERAN FLY-IN PILOTS

Ernie Hautala of Ely

*Dusty Rhodes, a B-5 Ryan, and
Hoot Gets off the Ground*

Hoot's Longest Fly-In Trip

Anecdotes from Hoot

Warroad's Don Hanson

Duck Soup at Sandy Beach

Big Walleyes on the Ice at 17-mile Reef

The Ice Fisherman with no Boots, Just Oxfords

*An Overturned Boat and a Mexican Strawhat:
Trouble on the Way to Oak Island*

77 LEO MANTHEI, BLACKDUCK GAME WARDEN

Largest Sheepshead from a Minnesota Lake?

"I-s T h a t Y o-u, L-e-o?"

80 G. H. NELSON

Trolling Out of Hovland: A Record Lake Trout

82 GORDON YAEGER, ON WHITEWATER TROUT

From the Rochester Post-Bulletin

85 TERRY FUSSY'S RECORD CHANNEL CAT,
AND PRAISING THE MISSISSIPPI

87 F. H. "MAC" McARDLE, PELICAN RAPIDS WARDEN

*Spearers Encounter Warden Bob Streich –
Buried in the Sand!*

Loudmouth Bay

Poachers at Little Pine Lake

Walkie-Talkies and Fred Johnson's Cousin

Netting the Netters

93 *ROYAL KARELS, BASSMASTER*

　　Shooting Down a Shakespeare Mouse

　　Bass Plugs Fly on Rabbit Lake: "Waylaying the Old Man"

　　A Giant Bullfrog and Bass Near the Boat

　　Peter Miravelle and Royal Karels,
　　Disaster-prone Bassing Duo?

101 RON WEBER, THE RAPALA MAN

　　"They're Using that Finnish Plug":
　　Ron Weber Meets the Rapala

　　With Ray Ostrom and Upperman Bucktails:
　　Rapalas on Trial at Mille Lacs

107 A STURGEON RECORD, ANYBODY?

　　That Old 236-pound Sturgeon "Record"

　　225-pound Sturgeon Found Dead in Rush Lake

　　176-pound Sturgeon from White Earth Lake,
　　Becker County, "Killed in Shallow Water"

　　A 162-1/2-pound "Rainy River" Sturgeon: Hook 'n Line?

115 DICK PENCE, WHIPHOLT GUIDE

　　Smelt or Shmelt?

　　A Flight to Grand Rapids for Billy Fins

　　Tyin' Knots

118 CLIFF RIGGLES, CASS LAKE GUIDE

　　A Favorite Guiding Trip on Cass Lake

　　Big Muskie Catches Angler with Pants Down

　　Cliff's Biggest Muskie

125 CLARENCE LUTHER, GUIDE FOR 60 YEARS

　　"I've Never Fallen In"

Fred Potthoff's Big Walleyes

Gangsters and Machine Guns

A Day with Doctor Dewey

130   GARY KORSGADEN, "CRAPPIE KING"

Murky Water, Gapen's Cockroach, and Giant Crappies

Playing Hooky, and an Unexpected Meeting with the Principal at Little Toad Lake

136   STAN NELSON, FROM LITCHFIELD

Little Green Frogs and Big Bass at Ripley Lake

The Three Stooges at Manuella

The Tail End of a Tornado at Green Lake

143   A NEW STATE RECORD MUSKIE— 19 YEARS AFTER THE CATCH!

Art Lyons and His Record Muskie: An Account of What Happened

More on Art Lyons' 54-pound Muskie

151   CHARLIE JANNI, RIVER RAT

Clam Fishin' on the Minnesota River

Fishing Walleyes at Reim's Camp

Trotlines in the River

159   GENE SHAPINSKI, UNORTHODOX ANGLER

A Deal with Towner: Trading Fish for Meat

Catching a Northern Pike on Another Northern

Meyer Lake Northern Hits Bass and Runs

A Pack of "Wolves" in Wolf Lake?

18-pound Northern Jumps into Boat

165   ART BARNEVELD, LAUNCH SKIPPER

Flatfish 'n' Worm Days

A Wallet on Ice

Poundage

171   JERRY FULLER OF PARK RAPIDS

Fuller's, and the Longest-running
Fishing Contest in Minnesota

Contest Cheating: A "Clank" on the Scale!

A Trophy Belle Taine Smallmouth

Big Browns from the Straight River and Straight Lake

Fuller's Guides, Including Sy Siebert

A Fish Hook Lake Northern
That Never Made It to Town

Jim Heddon: Spurning Outboard Motors and Live Bait

178   MINNESOTA TV FISHING, 1950's STYLE

Stu Mann's "Minnesota Outdoors," as Stu Remembers

Catching Bass in Mid Air:
Stu Mann Versus Leo Pachner

Rollie Johnson, WCCO, Corrie's,
and a Fishing Contest

Warmath, Corrie, VanKonynenburg, and Johnson:
Shooting the Rapids with a "Touch of the Lord"

187   GERHARDT BLOCK, "MR. WALLEYE"

Hellcats and Lunker Walleyes on Big Stone Lake—
How it All Started

Cussin' the Carp

Gerhardt's Introduction to Pimple Fishin'

Lunker Walleyes Through the Ice at Big Stone:
Some Blockbuster Hits

194 BUD DENNY, FROM BENA ON BIG WINNIE

Walleyes: A Cure for Sea Sickness?

Terrific Winnie Walleye Fishing

High Stakes

A Big One that Got Away

Dunkings off Raven's Point

In a Storm off High Banks

199 JIMMY ROBINSON, A FISHERMAN TOO

Governor Freeman and Old Tony

Opening Day but No Fishing for Jimmy

Fishing Years Ago Around Perham

Jimmy Robinson's Eagle Lake Muskie

205 GENE JENKINS, LAKE VERMILION GUIDE

A Stream of Bubbles Goin' Up the River

Price's Stretch: People from Kansas City Go Down the Chute

The Trout Lake Portage and Across Vermilion at Midnight

212 BABE WINKELMAN, PRO FISHERMAN

Wading the Mississippi, When a Smallmouth Changed Course

A Bass Fisherman's Dream "Near St. Cloud"

219 A MINNESOTA LUNKER LIST

About the Author

From opening day in May to the middle of October, Joe Fellegy, fishing guide since a teenager, is on Mille Lacs Lake seven days a week helping folks catch walleyes.

Joe is an avid storyteller and lover of fishing stories, and this book reflects his deep interest and joy in fishing. He closely identifies with fishermen, young and old, who make up Minnesota's most popular sport.

In the winter months, at his cabin on the shore of his favorite lake, Joe writes for regional and national outdoor magazines—when he isn't ice fishing. Joe is a graduate of St. John's University (Collegeville) and a member of the Outdoor Writers Association of America. He is also the author of *Walleyes and Walleye Fishing*.

Introduction

This is a story book which departs from the usual how-to and where-to in today's fishing literature. *Classic Minnesota Fishing Stories* is anything but another fishing bible, encyclopedia, guide, or manual which catalogs guaranteed "best methods" and "expert advice." Instead, my purpose here is to capture in print those alive qualities of fishing—action, excitement, and the human element—in the familiar setting of Minnesota's lakes and streams.

Countless fishing books, articles, and columns teem with instructions and tips aimed at helping us catch more and bigger fish under all conceivable conditions. This business of in-depth fishing education began booming its way across the United States in the early 1970's and continues to grow. Manufacturers refine tackle and accessories. And fishing experts inject the once contemplative sport with increasing doses of science and system. These days, everybody's imitating the pros and pursuing the "facts" of fishing.

Often lost in this frenzied quest for expertise is one of fishing's most precious treasures, that special flavor of it all which figures so strongly in our enjoyment of fishing. I mean that rich blend of people, places, moods, and happenings on the water which make fishing trips worth remembering.

Aspects of this dynamic side of fishing are preserved and passed on to others through a kind of folklore, the fishing story. The telling of fishing stories is largely an oral tradition, most of it going unrecorded. Indeed, most fishing stories seldom escape an inner circle of friends, relatives, and fishing companions. Because of their intimacy with the sport's action and color, veteran anglers are frequently the most entertaining tellers of fishing stories. Unfortunately, many of our best stories die with old guides and all kinds of interesting fishing people.

The stories in this book sample Minnesota's finest fishing lore. Most of them are first-hand accounts, straight from the mouths of

1

seasoned guides, local fishing veterans, pro fishermen, outdoor media people, and others with colorful angling experiences. Their narrations vary considerably in content, language, and style, reflecting diverse backgrounds and interests. A good share of the stories are action-packed, recounting thrilling episodes on lake and river. Some recall spectacular fishing history. Yet others zero in on the humorous, the unusual, and even some commonplace happenings— the kind that initiate good talk wherever fishing people meet.

Most readers who fish in Minnesota will recognize at least some of the story tellers. Guides like Harry Van Doren and Clarence Luther of Nisswa, Art Barneveld at Mille Lacs, Bud Denny from Big Winnie, and Cass Lake's Cliff Riggles will long be remembered as personalities who lent a certain sparkle to the Minnesota fishing scene. Al Lindner's reputation as a skilled fisherman stretches nationwide. Actually, every story teller in this book has left some kind of mark on sport fishing in Minnesota. Chances are you'll be acquainted with many of the waters where their stories take place.

Some of the reminiscences in this book take us back a few years. Charlie Janni, Charlie Isle, Jimmy Robinson, and other old-timers bring angling history to life in a magical way with their stories of how it was years ago. In places you may feel a tinge of nostalgia while recalling an era when a favorite hot lure made its biggest splash!

In the stories of some old-timers there is the recurring theme of angling and spearing fish by the sackful, or even by the wagon-load! There seems to have been fishing in season and out of season, inside and outside the law—if there was a law. By no means are any accounts in this book meant to endorse or promote extra-legal fishing activities. One must view the stories in the context of their times. In some cases sport fishing was in its infancy, when fishing pressure was negligible and before much of a fishing ethic had evolved. Many of yesterday's "outlaws" are leading conservationists today!

The stories of state record fish included here take on special significance as long-standing Minnesota records are reviewed and sometimes challenged. The tossing out of J. W. Collins' Lake of the Woods muskie as a record in 1976, after 45 years of champion status, spurred a new interest in the validity of records which had stood for years.

I must address the matter of language used by story tellers in this book. It seems that fishing people, including college graduates and VIPs, talk fishing with an informal and relaxed lingo. You'll find exceptions, but when fishing becomes the topic of conversation many anglers, whether consciously or not, shift from a more disciplined English to a looser fishtalk. Grammarians and students of syntax may cringe at some of their unstructured ramblings.

But these affronts to linguistic propriety must be accepted here. Why quibble about the simple and natural usage that fishing people know so well? To say that fish were "taken with consistency" or that "the harvest was bountiful" hardly measures up to "We clobbered 'em" or "They really nailed 'em!"

This book features the more familiar fishing vernacular used by the various story tellers. In editing this collection, my concern was to preserve as much as possible the language and spirit of each of them. I believe that is why their stories show off a refreshing and unmanufactured character. They are true originals.

Some call the misspelling of one's name the "ultimate discourtesy." Despite my extraordinary efforts, there may be a mistake or two. Sincere apologies!

The fishing stories brought together here grow out of the impressive diversity and richness of Minnesota's fishing heritage. Perhaps no other state can offer the gamut of freshwater sport fishing found here—from brook trout to lake trout, from bluegills to muskies, from catfish in a lazy prairie river to crappies beneath the ice of a snow-covered northern lake.

Taste fishing's flavor! Have fun with *Classic Minnesota Fishing Stories.*

Harry Van Doren, Nisswa Guide

Around Nisswa, Minnesota, Harry Van Doren is as legendary as the lakes he guided on for 58 years. Those familiar with fishing on Edward, Gull, Pelican and other lakes in that region invariably know of the colorful Van Doren. He started his nearly six decades of guiding in 1920 at the age of 11. His mother rented three cabins and some boats on Lake Edward, so it seems natural that young Harry got into the fishing business.

Harry Van Doren's First Guiding Trip

My first trip for hire that I clearly recall was on the bass opener in June of 1920. I was only a kid then, about 11 years old. On that occasion a guy by the name of Harry Wanger and his wife from Duluth came down to our place on Lake Edward. It was four in the morning when they woke my mother up. She woke me up and said I should take them fishing.

I used a flat-bottomed boat that my dad built. It was fairly windy so it got to be pretty tough rowing. We had gone out at five in the morning so I was kind of bushed by the time we got in at noon.

We ate dinner and got back on the lake by no later than 1:30. We fished all afternoon. The limit then was 15 bass. The guy's wife had her 15, but he had 13 and wasn't about to quit until he got two more. Guess he didn't want his wife to beat him! So we kept on fishing. Along with those bass we had a stringer of northerns—I don't know how many—but they were draggin' heavy alongside the boat.

Finally, it got so dark he gave up without catching those last two bass. When we got into shore I was really woofed out. We got the fish in their car and the gear racked up, and he asked me, "What do I owe you?"

I told him it was a dollar for the boat, and before I could say

5

any more he said, "Well, it don't make any difference anyway because I only have two dollars!"

So I got a whole dollar for that hard day's work! I kidded Harry's son with that story and he said he didn't know his old man was a cheapskate. Of course that was a long time ago.

Harry's Best Season on Gull Lake

1958 was probably the best year Gull ever had, at least as far as I can recall. At that time I rented a boat from McMaster's Resort all summer. I didn't keep track, but the McMasters did. That August, in 30 days, I brought in 900 walleyes. That was guiding with two customers in the boat, two trips per day. There was nothing under three pounds and some over ten. That year the catch for my boat was 2,305 walleyes.

We fished mostly with minnows. We did some fishing with Little Joe Spinners and nightcrawlers, but the good catches of big walleyes were made on minnows—suckers mainly, but some chubs. That August fishing started out in about 15 feet. But as the season went on into September and the water cooled, we got down as deep as 50 to 55 feet.

There were plenty of outstanding trips that year. I remember one time I took out Doc Lyons of Clinton, Iowa. He had been going out with another guide, but couldn't catch a walleye. So he got wind of my good luck with the big walleyes and decided to hire me to take him out one morning. So I took my boat from McMaster's and headed over to Sandy Point Resort where Doc stayed.

By the time I got over there the waves were four feet high. He and his wife were both supposed to go, but she looked out at the lake and flatly refused. He asked me if I was sure I wanted to go. I said sure I'm going out. It was the kind of weather the walleyes liked. So he went and woke one of the boys up and the three of us went out. After we got out there I found that Doc hadn't learned much from his other guide. I had to teach 'em from scratch. Well, it was rough and I had all I could do to keep the boat on the spot and watch their lines. It was up and down, up and down. I'd tell them when they had strikes and they wouldn't believe a fish was there. But when that boat went up and a rod tip didn't go up with it, I knew there was something at the other end. They'd set the hook and bring in big fish. I don't think we fished more than a couple hours. We came in with 18 walleyes that weighed 96 pounds.

Harry Van Doren, Nisswa guide for 58 years. He retired from his work at Marv Koep's Nisswa Bait Shop in 1978. (Photo by Carol Buckmann)

Another good trip was with Mrs. Baird Markham and her sister-in-law. He was a retired general who liked to fish. But his wife was crazy about fishing walleyes. So I took those gals over to Gull one morning. They were early birds. We got over there early, probably by six o'clock. It was all minnow fishing at the time.

By 10:30 we hadn't had the first strike! I decided to try one last place before giving up. I hit a school of walleyes and they were good ones! Between taking care of those two women—netting the fish and taking 'em off the hooks and baiting their hooks—I didn't get in much fishing, especially with fighting the boat in a pretty good wind. I didn't even have time to string the fish, they were coming in so fast.

Finally I said we had to quit until I could count the fish. I figured we had too many already. We did. There were 23 walleyes on the bottom of the boat, so I released five freshly-caught ones. We didn't weigh the whole string, but those gals had three 10-pounders in that catch!

Young Harry Jumps in and Swims Home

I was maybe 14 or 15 years old. We had a salesman from the Walnetto Candy Company that came up and rented one of my mother's cabins on Lake Edward. Sometimes he'd bring a whole group of salesmen up here for a weekend of fishing.

I had this guy out fishing one morning. It was windy, a south wind, and we were fishing bass at the north end of the lake. In order to hold the boat so he could cast to the edge of the reeds I had to keep the bow almost straight into the wind.

The only thing he'd fish with was a Heddon #210, a surface bait with a silver metal collar that sticks out about a quarter of an inch around the head. It's a wide bait, one you can throw right into rushes and it'll come through because the body's so wide and the hooks are underneath.

I never wore a cap back then because my hair was pretty long. Every time he'd swing back for a cast—he'd have a foot and a half or two feet of line beyond the rod tip—he'd hook me in the hair. And that hurt! So I finally got mad and told him, "You're gonna have to wind that line up closer or cast at a little different angle." Cuz I was hurtin'!

And right away he answered back. "If you'd hold that boat around cross-ways to the wind I wouldn't have to cast that way!"

I said you can't do it. It's impossible. He insisted it could be done. So I told him to try it himself. Then I dove over the side, swam to shore, and walked home!

1955 Leech Lake Muskie Rampage

In the hot mid summer of 1955, on the weekend of July 16-17 and for the next few days, big Leech Lake muskies went on a hitting binge that will never be forgotten. An occasional fishing article still alludes to that exciting action. And pictures of those fantastic strings perennially find their way into Leech Lake promotional literature. But many of today's anglers have never read a detailed report of the historic "Muskie Rampage."

The scene of the action was the Two Points area of Portage Bay, Leech Lake's northeast arm. On July 16, a Saturday, 19 muskies were brought into Federal Dam. On Sunday, the total was 31. That weekend's catch of 51 ran from 18 to over 40 pounds. By Saturday, July 23, the number of muskies brought into Federal Dam probably exceeded 100.

Young Chuck Neururer had a 25-pounder; Bob Neururer, a 35-pounder; Pete Neururer, a 30-pounder. Jerry Bader took a 40-pounder, one of the top catches. Many of the fish were in that 25 to 40-pound class.

The five Federal Dam launch services operating at that time—Warren Bridge's Landing, Neururer's, Spillman's, Westcott's, and the Federal Dam Boat Livery—gave the walleyes a rest, and concentrated on muskie fishing during the peak period.

The following recollections of the 1955 muskie bonanza come from Garry Neururer, who, along with his brothers Bob and Pete, operated Neururer's Launch Service at Federal Dam for more than three decades. After muskies, Garry talks walleyes.

Garry Neururer Remembers the 1955 Leech Lake Muskie Rampage

In mid summer of 1955 we had about a two-week period of real hot and calm weather. It had been dry, too. During this time is when the muskies hit. Somebody came in with a muskie. Then more went out and tried it. And, by golly, they really started hittin'! It went on as long as the weather stayed that way. When the winds came up again the muskie fishin' was over for awhile and we went back to walleyes.

Once the word got out a lot of people tried for muskies. The action was all over in Portage Bay, up by Two Points. There would be 85 to 100 boats over there, at least that many. So you see, it wasn't a lake-wide thing. There was a strip, a weedbed along the shore, maybe a half-mile wide and probably three or four miles long. You could fish it back and forth. You could look out there about any time, with all those boats out there, and see somebody tangling with a muskie!

Now before this muskie thing started, we had been going about our walleye fishing as usual. But the walleyes had been slowing down about the time those muskies got started, so the Federal Dam launches began making muskie trips. It wasn't long before

A wheelbarrow load of 1955 Leech Lake muskies. Longtime Federal Dam launch operator Garry Neururer is at the handles. Others are (left to right) Ralph Hewitt, Des Moines; Walter Kreutner, Shellsburg, IA; and Bob Neururer.

10

guides and other folks from all over Leech Lake were coming up here to Portage Bay for muskies. During the height of that muskie fishing I can't remember anybody fishing for walleyes. The muskies stole the whole show for probably a week to ten days.

The peak of this muskie "rampage" lasted, I'd say, three to four days. Then pretty good fishing went beyond that. It was during those several peak days when that famous picture of the string of muskies was taken, along with the wheelbarrow load. A 42-1/2-pounder was the biggest one caught that time.

Some people did really well. There was a Jim Lucas from Remer, for instance. He had three straight days of fine muskie fishing. Hank Bloom from Remer was another one. A lot of people caught fish.

Back then it was heavy on trolling for the muskies, especially from the launches. But there was some casting too. They used all kinds of baits, everything like K-B and Doctor spoons, big plugs, bucktails—anything they could get, because this fishing took everyone by surprise. There wasn't that much tackle around! But I think the jointed Pikie Minnow was a little better than the rest.

As I said, the best fishing was in Portage Bay, the west side of the bay. The fish were caught mainly from 7 to 9 feet of water, in the weeds, and even from 15 to 18 feet along the drop-off near the edge of the weeds. But most of 'em were caught in the weeds. We were pulling weeds all the time.

There were a few northerns being caught in between the muskies, but not many. It was just about all muskies. And they were big fish, a lot of them between 30 and 40 pounds. If you came into a dock with a muskie that weighed 15 or 18 pounds, the people would look and say, "Oh, he's just a small one." Then they'd walk away to the next dock to inspect another boat!

The launches, the bigger boats, caught their share of muskies. I had muskies pretty near every trip I made. Many times I had two or three in a half day. One day I had only three people in the launch, so I went up to the office to get my wife and the two kids to go along. That afternoon the three guests caught three muskies that totalled 104 pounds! They were from Nebraska, two men and a woman staying at Judd Daniels' place on Winnie.

I remember that gal was always hollering about being tired of pulling her plug through the weeds. So she'd quit for "rest" periods while she monkeyed around. Then every once in a while she'd grab the pole and fish. Well, you know, she caught two muskies that afternoon! I remember we'd hold up a white flag on the way to the dock if there was a muskie in the boat. That time the kids held up three white flags!

Author's note: The news of a Leech Lake "muskie rampage" travelled fast—once it got out. Mrs. Neururer recalls: "It was on a Sunday when they really started biting. We called WCCO in Minneapolis and they sort of laughed at us. And then finally, when we had all those muskies at the docks, we got a hold of the Grand Rapids paper. They came over and took that big group picture with all the guides. We called a number of newspapers, but Grand Rapids was the only one that came over.

"The pictures look impressive. But, you know, a lot of the people took their muskies and left right away. Many fish were never photographed."

Stu Mann, an outdoor writer with a TV outdoor show in the Twin Cities, witnessed some of that hot muskie fishing. He took his movie camera along on the launch and got a whole reel of muskie fishing. He just made it to the dock when I was about ready to pull out. The rest of the launches were already gone. He wanted to go, along with his partner, a fellow from the Creek Chub lure company. So I told them they could ride along to take movies and try out plugs.

And I got them up to launches, I don't know how many times, when somebody was bringing in a muskie. I could always tell if they were fighting a fish because when they hit a muskie they'd shut the motor off and quit trolling until they got the fish in. So he got film of muskies being fought, gaffed, and brought in.

I remember Stu Mann saying, "Now if we could get a big muskie on this boat we'd have 'er made." A few minutes later a guy on our boat hooked one. So he got a film of it, all the while the guy was fightin' it and letting it go, and bringing it in again. And he also got a shot of me reaching down with the gaff and hoisting it up over the side of the boat. I'm pretty sure that fish weighed 37 pounds!

I told those guys they'd probably never see anything like that again. My god! A half a day and see that many muskies come in?

We had spurts of action in years after that, when the weather and conditions got right. I remember a couple years after that 1955 fishing when we had a warm spell and calm weather. We were fishin' walleyes in Portage Bay, but we had this bunch from

25 of the 51 silver muskies caught out of Federal Dam, Minnesota on Leech Lake, July 16 and 17, 1955. Pictured with the fish are (left to right) Warren Bridge, Guy Fowlon, Frank Condon, Harold Bridge, Bob Neururer, Garry Neururer, Bob Chalich, Dan Chalich, Al Bader, George Durkee, Cal West-cott, Warner Spillman, Merle Westcott, Frank Clemas, and Smiley Cloud.

Iowa that came into the place and wanted to go muskie fishin'. So they were out there in one of our launches after muskies. I was ready to take another launch out with a load of walleye fishermen.

My nephew Charlie—they called him Chuck—was about 15 then. Now he's quite a muskie fisherman. Anyway, he wanted to go muskie fishin'. But all the rowboats were gone, and the muskie launch trip with those Iowa guys was already out. So I asked him to jump in with me and to take his muskie plugs along. After all, we were going walleye fishin' on the old muskie grounds.

"Aw," he said, "I'll never get any muskies that way." But he jumped in and came along. You know, he sat up in the front of the launch casting for muskies while the rest were fishin' for walleyes. And he brought in two nice muskies! And there were plenty of others that followed his lures right up to the boat. There you had muskies and walleyes together!

Lazy Ikes and Brooks Reefers at Leech

There was a guy up here from Iowa, back in about 1948. He brought a couple Lazy Ikes along on a launch trip. They made those lures in Fort Dodge, Iowa.

13

When this guy was here, the walleyes weren't hittin' too good on minnows. So he told us he had a couple new baits along that he wanted to try. And try 'em he did. He caught nearly all the fish! And of course you couldn't get any Lazy Ikes around here. Everybody was excited.

Now, I don't remember where he stayed, somewhere by Longville maybe. Anyhow, the next day he came back with some more lures. In the meantime we got some over at Grand Rapids. These were all different colors and it didn't make a whole lot of difference. The walleyes hit on all of them. We trolled kind of fast, and when they hit the Lazy Ike they were hooked! Everybody went for Lazy Ikes after that day.

A couple or three years after that we started plug fishing with Brooks Reefers. I picked one up, an orange jointed one. That seemed to work okay so we got some more. Now that was fishing 'em plain—no nightcrawlers or anything—with a fairly heavy sinker and a gut leader at least three feet long. You needed that gut leader so the plug could work better. We moved pretty fast with the Reefers.

I remember trips when the oldtime fishermen wanted to stick with their minnows, but before the trip was over they'd be dragging plugs. I remember many trips when everybody on the boat used Brooks Reefers.

July and August were the two best months for that plug fishing. And, on top of catching fish, there were real advantages with those plugs. For one thing, we used less minnows and saved there. And we didn't have to wait for the kind of rough water that made minnow fishin' good. With those Ikes and Reefers you could get by when things were dead calm.

Cal Backer's Trophy

The True Story of Cal Backer's Trophy Catch

A 212-pound Rainy Lake Guide on a Dardevle

Cal Backer of New Ulm, Minnesota did the unthinkable. He surely experienced that heavy feeling of having goofed when he heard a shout and then saw his Dardevle hanging from the husky guide's nose. It was hardly the trophy he expected to catch on his trip to Rainy Lake with the New Ulm Fishing Club!

For the story of Cal's unusual catch, I talked with several members of the club, including Mr. Backer himself. Here are their recollections.

Cal Backer: I was with a bunch of guys from New Ulm on an annual fishing trip. This particular year we rented one of Northern-aire's houseboats on Rainy Lake. We headquartered on that big houseboat, but we'd fish in small boats, two of us to a boat. And there were guides.

On this trip were Don Gollnast, the banker; Frank Carthey, a doctor; Warren "Schmaltz" Marti of Schell's Brewery; Dr. Charlie Hintz, a dentist; Don Alsop, who later became a federal judge; Denny Warta, the soft water man; Carl "Red" Wyszawski, the clothier who became Mayor of New Ulm; and myself.

Don Gollnast: It was early in the fishing season, in May. It was cold! The houseboat was in Canadian waters of Rainy Lake, not far from a portage to Sawbill Lake. Charlie Hintz and I fished walleyes on Rainy, but the rest of the guys portaged up to Sawbill. Charlie and I filled out on walleyes, and the others did so-so. What happened with Cal Backer and the guide took place on Sawbill Lake toward the beginning of our trip. In fact, I think it was on the first day.

15

Cal Backer: We were casting for northerns—Doc Carthey, myself, and our guide, who ran the motor. This one time I was getting ready to cast, went back with my rod, and as I made my cast I hooked our big guide right squarely through the tip of his nose!

Denny Warta: Schmaltz Marti and I were fishing in another boat, a little ways away. We didn't see it happen, but we were sitting there fishing when all of a sudden this boat comes by with Cal Backer in the middle, Doc Carthey up front, and this guide running the motor. And what a sight he was! The guide had blood pouring out of his nose, and that big long spoon was hanging there!

Marti hollered, "What in the hell are you using for bait, Cal?"

Doc didn't have a side-cutter with him, and it wasn't the right situation for working on him, so they went back to the houseboat.

Cal Backer: Now this Schmaltz Marti, being a born comedian, instigated what happened next. And the guide went along with it! We actually took the guide, tied a rope around his feet, and hoisted him up in the air. There he was, upside down, with my Dardevle

The Dardevle

Inventd by Lou J. Eppinger of Detroit in 1897; patented in 1905. Called the Osprey Spoon prior to 1918, then "Dare-Devil" after a World War I fighting unit. Some clergymen objected to "devil," hence the present "Dardevle."

hanging from his nose! I stood next to him with my fishing rod, the way they pose with big sailfish or marlin down south. Then pictures were taken of me and my "trophy."

Doc Carthey thought it would be best to get the guy into town. So he was taken into Fort Frances, Ontario to get my hook out of his nose. That night he came back, feeling very happy. He apparently had been drinking something other than a prescribed medicine. He was bombed!

We felt the whole thing was really funny, until sometime the next spring when I got sued! The guide wound up with $500 from my insurance company.

Anyway, I'm the one who caught a 212-pound guide on a Dardevle. And there are pictures to prove it!

Al Lindner

To many readers of this book, Al Lindner needs no introduction. One of the original "pro" fishermen, Al has gained fame as guide, tackle maker, tournament winner, author of fishing books, lecturer, star of several television fishing shows, and publisher of the *In Fisherman* magazine. Al and his brother Ron settled in the Brainerd, Minnesota area in the late 1960's.

Despite the glamorous side of his fishing career, Al Lindner must be characterized simply as a plain-speaking, jean-clad "die hard" who fishes whenever and wherever he can.

All About Landing A 44-Pound Mississippi River Muskie—On 6-pound Test Line!

It was on the Mississippi River, around the beginning of November, 1976. We were catching walleyes by the trillions below the dam at the paper mill in Brainerd. I'll never forget one of those fall trips.

Mort Bank, a friend of mine from Bismarck, North Dakota, and I patronized the same insurance agent, Bill Olmsted from Brainerd. The three of us had fished together a number of times. Anyway, this one day Mort came over to my office and asked if I had time to go fishing. I said, "Yeah, I got the boat and stuff here so we'll go this afternoon."

So after lunch we went down to the river. I must have had about six dozen minnows along for tipping on the backs of jigs. We went through those minnows so fast it would make your head spin! There was a hit on every cast. I had an anchoring position, in good relation to an eddy, which allowed us to cast to two points which produced fish all the time. If you got tired of casting on one side of the boat you could switch and hit the other point. There were fish on all over the place, but nothing good-sized.

We played with a couple other spots that had fish, but still no size. So a little before dark Mort wanted to try something different, to look for some bigger fish. We moved a little downstream from the dam, to the site of a discharge from the paper mill. It's "purified" stuff, but it has a different color and a distinct odor about it.

I dropped the anchor and right away on the first cast—bang! The walleyes were there. Well, Mort threw out his jig and right away thought he was snagged. He jerked around a few times but was still hung up. Then he thought he felt a slight throb on the line. About that time I looked at his rod and said, "Hey, you've got a fish on there!"

It didn't run. Didn't do nuthin'. It just started to swim up-current real nonchalant-like. Mort started to put on a little pressure. But he had only six-pound line on a spinning rod. All he could do was put a little pressure on that fish to see if it would stop. Then he'd have to backreel.

The fish moved upstream quite a distance before I decided to lift the anchor and run it down. My first thought was that it was a big redhorse snagged in the tail or the belly—or somethin' odd. I was cold and would have liked him to break the line off! It was getting pretty dark and we were about ready to leave anyway.

But Mort wanted to see the fish. So I lifted the anchor and followed his mystery fish with the motor. I'd get over the fish and then calmly make some casts and catch another walleye or two.

Well, Mort hooked the fish about five o'clock. For the next 10 minutes or so we never saw the fish because it just stayed down. Then we got into a boily area with lots of current and the fish made its first run. She peeled quite a bit of line off Mort's reel and then I saw the line comin' up. The fish came up out of the water quite a distance from us, going in the opposite direction, away from us. I saw part of the body and the tail. That's when I knew it wasn't a redhorse. I figured it was a good, good northern, maybe a 15 or 18 pounder, a darn nice fish. So I got a little excited and agreed that we better concentrate on getting this fish in the boat.

I started following it. She swam lazily through some of the backwater areas and finally came around the corner by the dam and got into that fast current. And we just blew right down with 'er, swirled around right by the dam. She came right around the

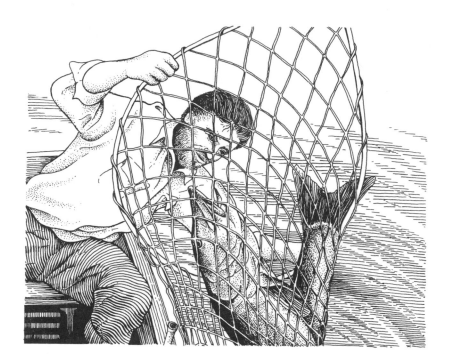

corner by a concrete wall that comes out there, and we drifted on down to an eddy. Then all of a sudden she popped up and we got a look. It was about 25 feet from the boat. I got really nervous then. I told Mort he had a muskie, and on top of that she looked like a good 30-pound fish.

The fish eased back down again, and we got to lookin' in the boat for something to land it with. But we had no net, no club, no gaff—nothing at all. Now what were we gonna do? We checked with a couple of shore fishermen, but they had a little net, way too small for this big fish.

I told Mort to let out line, hoping the fish would stay out in the main pool—'cuz there's a lot of snags in that river. The fish behaved okay, though, never getting nervous and never making big powerful runs.

Now, luckily, Bill was fishing from shore, on a little point. I told him to run to town to get us a big net. So he ran to the car, drove to Brainerd, and made it to Martin's Sport Shop downtown just as they were closing. He got a big net and flashlight, and soon returned to the river.

He came back to where he was before, where we had talked to

him. Problem was that in the meantime we had to follow the fish across the river. In order to get there Bill had to convince the security guard at the paper mill that he should be allowed through to get to us and our big fish. Finally the guard bought Bill's story and he got down to the water. We eased up to the bank and got the equipment into the boat.

The fish swam completely around the pool below the dam and stopped in the area where we hooked it. She then bulldogged right down to the bottom. I told Mort not to put pressure on it, just to let it sit there. There were snags nearby and I didn't want the fish to get nervous there. We didn't know what kind of shape that line was in. There wasn't much thickness there to begin with! She was hooked on the edge of the mouth, something I saw when she popped up that first time.

While Bill was gone to get the net, we had the fish near the boat a couple times, laying a few feet from us. I thought about getting my hands under it, but then chickened out. With 6-pound line, one mistake would have been the end. I knew that with a big net we could get it, so I didn't want to spoil things. We'd just leave 'er sit there and wait.

About 15 minutes after we got the landing net, Mort put pressure on the fish and she came up. I laid the net under the big thing. She was pretty beat and just shook a couple times. I pulled the net toward me so I could grab the hoop. I didn't trust the handle because that fish was heavy!

She rolled a few times in the boat, and that was it. Mort's muskie was fat as a pig. It had probably feasted on those little walleyes below the dam, and it had a 2-1/2 or 3-pound northern in its belly. In the boat I figured her for 35 pounds. But on the meat scale at the Baxter Store it weighed 44 pounds and 1 ounce.

The Lure Changer From St. Louis

One of the strangest things that ever happened to me on a fishing trip occurred back in the late 1960's when I was guiding out of Marv Koep's Nisswa Bait Shop. This trip was on North Long Lake, in September. I had been catching bass consistently, real, real regular. It was a variety of depths, but most of the time I was drop-off fishing.

In 1968 the term "structure," which everybody throws around today, was in its infancy. At that time I was part of a small group of people nationwide that avidly followed the structure concept to the penny. I went by the book, just hounding the drop-offs. In my mind, if you didn't fish this way you didn't catch no fish! And it was working for me. I was catching lots of fish.

Bass at this time of the year, according to most theories, were deep and fishing was tough. That sort of idea was floatin' around. But I used to fish a 6-inch jig-worm, the High Tail worm made by the Marlin Bait Co. in Indiana, and a spinnerbait called Lang's Raider. I'd work the edges of those drop-offs. At that time my style of fishing for those bass was quite an accomplishment. I fished bunches of deep-water bass on North Long that had never seen baits to any extent, because almost all the bass fishing on that lake was done by frog fishermen in the reeds.

So I had been doin' real good, and I had a group out from Pott-hoff's, a resort where I pulled the majority of my bass guiding parties. They were two guys from St. Louis, but I don't recall their names. Now there might be somewhat of a seasonal movement. I'm not sure. I do know that in September and October the Merri-field end of North Long produces one heck of a lot of bass. That's where I planned to go, because there wasn't a lot of action in the main lake at this time, and the #371 end wasn't doing much either. But the public access was on the #371 end.

So I came down from Koep's, put my boat in there, and I just knew that when I'd get up to the other end of the lake I'd find 10, 12, or 15 bass in my four-hour run. I wasn't worried about that. These guys were kind of new around there, a first-time guiding group for me. They weren't regulars. So I decided to fish my way up the lake, to check three or four spots on the way up there, just to see if there was any activity. I had a couple of big fish holes that every once in a while would produce a 4, 4-1/2, or a 5-pound bass. I knew I'd find 'em enough action sooner or later.

So I started to fool around like that, moving up the lake. I hit one spot and no fish. Two spots and no fish. Three spots and no fish. I got to the fourth spot, the narrows between the big part of North Long and the area they call the Merrifield end. It's a deep channel area where the drop-offs really fall, like from four feet to thirty feet immediately, just as if you gouged it out. There's a little tiny point that comes in there and it usually has a fish or two in it. So I pulled in there and was just gonna fish this point before going to the upper part of the lake.

By this time the guy in the middle of the boat was getting bored. We had fished maybe an hour and a half, hit several spots, and we hadn't had a strike yet. We were all fishing the same way, with those jig-worms and spinnerbaits, holding the boat in deep-water and throwing up onto the drop-off, then working the baits down these shelves.

So this guy was getting antsy, and he turned out to be one of those "lure changers." (Only a guide can truly appreciate this!) I told him his baits wouldn't work. But he'd make three casts with a lure, and then he's back to something else. He's rummaging through his tackle box and I'm thinking to myself as I'm workin' this point, "I've got one of these guys again." I figured in the next half hour, in the next spot, we'd catch some fish and he'd go back

to something that works. Maybe he'll get fortunate and get one or two, but the other guy'll probably catch the fish. This was all goin' through my mind. And the guy's coming out with a few remarks here and there.

So I continue down the side of this point. I'm backtrolling and casting, and occasionally I look in his tackle box. He didn't have much to choose from, not for this kind of fishing. He had all the old, old standbys—a bunch of Dardevles, Johnson spoons, a couple Jitterbugs, a few Hula-Poppers, and some Flatfish—the basic mainstay baits. I'm lookin' in there and thinkin' to myself, "How in the hell is he gonna catch a fish in this kind of depth on any of the baits he's got there? What could he possibly put on next?"

Well, he snaps on an average-size Jitterbug, a black Jitterbug, a noisy surface bait. And I'm thinkin, "Oh, my God! Of all choices!" He turns around in the boat and doesn't throw toward the drop-off. Instead he turns around the opposite way and makes a cast right square into the middle of the channel, over 30 feet of water! With a Jitterbug!

He doesn't make five turns with the damn reel handle, and bang! He gets a strike and catches a bass about 2-1/2 pounds. This just about blew my mind! He reels it in, puts it in the boat, and I concede that "strange things do happen." Then he makes another cast and catches another bass! And then another! So the other guy and I put on top-water baits and we caught 13 nice bass suspended over the center of that channel, scattered over 30 feet of open nothing—no drop-offs, no cover! I still don't know what those fish were doin' there or where they were goin' to.

That happening made a big impact on my fishing thinking. There is no one way to catch fish. The fish go wherever they want to go, when they want to go there. It opened my mind. I moved away from that hard-core attitude—"This is the only way to fish."

I've been back there many times and have thrown a variety of baits over the deep water in that channel, and I've never taken another largemouth bass there! I probably stopped there 50 times in the next few years. But I have caught bass suspended out over the middle of nowhere, on a number of lakes, especially in the fall during the turnover time or shortly after the turnover. Now, with some regularity, I can go out and fish with baits two, three, and four feet down over 25, 30, or 35 feet of water, like off of points, and catch largemouth bass. But I'll never forget that lure changer, when he turned his back on the drop-off and started throwing that Jitterbug.

Hjalmar Swenson, A Fisheries Chief

For many years, the name Hjalmar Swenson was synonymous with Minnesota fisheries. Swenson's career in fisheries spanned 46 years, starting fulltime in 1928. Before that, he worked seasonally for five years at the Bemidji walleye spawning stations and hatchery.

Hjalmar worked his way up through the ranks to become Supervisor of Fisheries in 1946, a post he held until retirement in 1973.

Swenson Short Stories

I took in many interesting meetings in my time, some hot and some cold. And there was the endless stream of letters and petitions. I recall one letter that was special. The party criticized the whole Department of Natural Resources and its activities. But then the last sentence read something like this: "Well, keep up the good work, and don't let these crackpots bother you."

That letter was passed around the Department, I guess to see who would take the first crack at it. I answered by saying that the letter, particularly the last sentence, was much appreciated!

Bad fishing doesn't always mean a low fish population. Back in the summer of 1957, when walleye fishing was down on one of the major lakes, some resorters insisted that "something has to be done." They thought the walleye population was depleted. They suggested a new fish hatchery, or maybe a new supervisor of fisheries!

But the following winter the walleye fishing there was fantastic, and the same resort people wanted the season closed because fishermen were catching "too many fish!"

In the early 1950's, when we realized it was time to restrict the take of lake trout, we reduced the possession limit from 10 to 5. Some resort people told the DNR commissioner that if Swenson had something to do with this move he should be replaced. They complained that they'd have to close shop if they couldn't send their customers home with 10 trout.

To that I said they might as well start packing up, as some day they would have to settle for less.

Many years ago, when I stopped at a fishing camp, a group of out-of-staters had just laid out their catch of northern pike. They were arguing about which ones were northerns and which ones were pickerel. They asked me to take a look. I said, "They're all northern pike."

"That's good," one fellow said. "I don't like those darn pickerel anyway."

You know, there are no true pickerel in Minnesota!

A "one hour afternoon catch off the dock" at Le Clair, Lake of the Woods, in 1901. Bronco Bill and Postmaster. (Minnesota Historical Society)

When Something Big Entered The Trap at Waskish

In April of 1941 I was staying part time at the new walleye hatchery on the Winter Road River at Baudette. That was a political hatchery that should never have been built.

This one night, that April, while on my way from St. Paul to Baudette, I stopped at the Waskish spawning station on the Tamarac River to see how the walleye run was going. It was about midnight. The nets were filling up with fish and all looked okay to Buckshot Joe, the night man there.

When I came back there the next morning there were school buses and people all over the place. You see, soon after I had left there, after midnight, something big came into the trap and started pushing the traps and platforms around. So Joe woke up the crew and told them that something big was in there. He said it looked like a pig and sounded like a beaver!

Well, here was a big rock sturgeon! I measured it and weighed it. It was 6 feet 4 inches long, 29 inches around the head, and it weighed 142 pounds. After pictures, I attached a cattle tag, #99, to the gill cover and turned the big fish loose.

A few weeks later when the fishing season opened, a fellow who was fishing in the rain, with an old cane pole, hooked onto something he couldn't lift from the bottom. So he pulled up his anchor. Then his boat was towed around near the mouth of the Tamarac River for several hours. Finally whatever he had broke loose. I'm presuming it was the big sturgeon, #99. That fish was never seen or heard of since, as far as I know.

Charlie Isle, Old-Timer

It seems like Charlie Isle has lived and fished all over Crow Wing County, the Cuyuna Range, and elsewhere in some of central Minnesota's richest lake and river country. Born in Nokay Lake Township, Crow Wing County, in 1898, Charlie knew fishing in Minnesota back when it was often for meat or for money, when limits were liberal and practically everything was considered "legal"!

Spearing on Borden and Mille Lacs, 1910

I came down to the Garrison area when I was 12 years old, in the spring of 1910. I stayed on Borden Lake for a week that time, with Joe Harrison. He was a farmer on Borden Lake, and the old house and barn are still there. Joe's daughter married Perry Borden and they lived at nearby Mille Lacs, on a farm near what is now Garrison Creek Marina. When we went to Mille Lacs, that's where we went.

During the day I'd help Joe with his farm work, and then at night we'd go fishin'. It was spearing, mainly on Borden and Mille Lacs. I loved that spearing at night. We'd have a big torch on the front of the boat. And the spear had a 16-foot handle. It was legal to spear anything. And I did. On Borden I speared sunfish, crappies, northerns, and bass. They weren't too big there, but they were nice fish.

Then one night this Joe Harrison said, "We'll go over to Perry's on Mille Lacs. Perry's brother, Leon Borden, was about my age. And we went out there on that lake, just the two of us. And man, I'm telling you!

We went out at the creek there, and went along the bay, down past where the drive-in theater is now, and down around where that big stone concourse goes out in the lake. Of course, none of that was there then. Leon and I both had spears and we'd sort of pole the boat along. With that light, and that sandy bottom, you could see those big northerns layin' around in there. I tell you, that was somethin' else!

I don't remember how many fish we got, but what we did get was nice fish. I don't suppose there was anything under 15 pounds.

Now that creek that comes into Borden Lake on the northeast corner flows from a rice bed and crosses Highway #18. It goes into Borden and then into Mille Lacs. Anyway, that same night, when we were comin' home—we had horses in those days—Mart Hill and someone else had been up on that creek all night. And you should have seen the fish they had!

They had a single light wagon. I s'pose the box was about 36 or 38 inches wide and probably about eight feet long. And that whole bed was laid up with those big northerns. They were just layin' tight in that box. I don't think there was anything under 15 to 20 pounds either. Oh, man. Nice fish!

They had been spearing all night. They had their fire on the bank so they could see.

I remember another time, when I was going to school at Esden, about six miles north of Garrison. The old road used to turn there and go south for a mile, then it went southeast again down around Scott Lake, down around Borden Lake, and then over to Garrison or "Midland." I saw something there one time. And this is no bull!

A guy who had a store in Garrison, right along there where the old hotel used to be, had four horses. There was a triple box on his wagon. And that was level full with northerns from Mille Lacs Lake! He was taking them to Brainerd. He'd peddle 'em in Brainerd. At that time one of the most popular spearing places around Mille Lacs was at Scguchio Crook, south of Garrison.

I speared there, too. We'd build a big fire on the bank so you could see. And them big old fish came down that creek. They looked like fence posts!

Fishin' The Mississippi

"Up From Brainerd"

I did a lot of fishin' on the Mississippi River, up from Brainerd, as far as Green's Point. I had a lot of interesting times on that river, going back to the days when they'd drive logs on it. We never did get really big walleyes up there, but we got a lot of good fish.

Where the Big Pine River goes into the Mississippi, a fella from Little Falls and I had a wanigan, a kind of houseboat. We lived on that boat, right on the river. We were pickin' deadheads up there, sunken logs. We were gettin' two-bits apiece for pickin' 'em. Those wages were paid by Parker-Kellog sawmill in Brainerd, the outfit that was sawing 'em up into lumber.

We used cedar rafts for loading those logs and hauling them to the mill. We kept the wanigan anchored in an eddy, tied to the shore. And we had set lines around the wanigan, baited with frogs. So we had walleyes to eat all the time. We caught walleyes, bass, and northerns on those lines—no junk fish.

That was about 1924. We averaged about $8.50, each one of us, per day—good money at that time. We didn't work more than six or seven hours a day, so we had plenty of time to hunt and fish.

I had a big smoke house when I lived at Nokay Lake. Actually, I built it as a chicken coop. But I never had any chickens! So I got a bunch of buffalo fish from the Mississippi River, for smoking.

That was something, too! There was a commercial fisherman over at Riverton. I won't say his name, 'cause he's liable to be alive yet. Anyway, he had 13 commercial nets in the river between Riverton and Brainerd. It was in March, and the river was starting to break up. He had these nets under the ice. They were big hoop nets, maybe 30 feet long, with wings for a long distance each way. The fish would follow those wings and funnel into the hoop net.

This was about the time beer was comin' back, in the 1930's. I think there was five of us that had a keg of beer over at Eagle Lake. We were drinkin' beer all night. And somebody said, "You know, it would be all right if we had some fish."

So my buddy said, "I know where there are some fish."

We were all feelin' pretty good and somebody hollered, "Yeah, let's go get some fish!"

Then we went up there to the river. We took a duck boat along for safety, to push out on the ice ahead of us. We cut each guy a sixteen-foot pole, in case we'd fall in. We got out there to one of those nets. And this is hard to believe, but I'll bet there were 20 ton of fish in that one gol damn net! There were so many fish in there that they had the ice all melted off over the top. It was loaded with buffalo. And there was everything else, too!

We had one small fella in the gang. We put him on a couple of poles and shoved him out there, and shoved the duck boat out

there. He filled the duck boat with those buffalo. And then he took about a gunny sack full of northerns, and about the same amount of walleyes. Then he opened the net and let the rest go, because the fish were crowded in there. The guy didn't empty that net soon enough.

So, we got back out to Eagle Lake and nobody wanted those buffalo. But I said, "I'll take the buffalo."

I had a hundred pounds of ice cream salt, so I cleaned those buffalo and salted 'em down. Then I used that chicken coop for a smokehouse. I put an old cook stove in there. And I was careful to put a big cover over the stove, to keep the direct heat away from the fish.

I cut the buffalo into chunks. And boy, did they turn out nice!

You know, nobody was around when we got those fish. Hell, we were messing with this guy's net and could have gotten into trouble! He was a licensed commercial fisherman, and a good guy. I like him a lot. He used to give us bullheads, but the gamefish all had to go back in the river. He was netting for buffalo, and I think they were shipped to Chicago or New York.

The Nokassippi Connection

The Nokassippi River runs out of Clearwater Lake, then into Eagle Lake, from Eagle Lake into Nokay Lake, and from Nokay into Heron Lake. Then it crosses Highway #18 and runs into South Long Lake, Lower South Long Lake, and into different lakes, and finally runs into the Mississippi River at Fort Ripley. I've fished a lot of those lakes.

I lived on Nokay Lake, twice in fact. The last time I lived there was during the Depression, when the mines on the Cuyuna Range were shut down. I was out of work and my kids were young.

We didn't have any boat, so I built a raft! My neighbors, the John Johnsons, gave me an old log house made of white pine, with the provision that I tear it down. I built the raft out of that. It was 26 or 28 feet long and maybe 10 feet wide. I put a deck on it, and we had chairs on it so the kids and everybody could fish. I borrowed an old boat to get the family out to the raft.

I used an old steel beam plow for an anchor, and anchored it right on the weedline. And we'd catch everything around that raft! Panfish, walleyes, northerns, bass—everything. We'd hoist 'em right up on the raft. But we never kept more than we wanted for a good mess of fish.

I'll tell you what I saw at Nokay Lake one spring night. A fella by the name of Tolefson, Clarence Tolefson, and I went out. He was doin' the paddling and I was doin' the spearing. That time I had a powder box with a looking glass in it, in the back, and a 2-burner Coleman. And boy, that's some kind of light!

We had a little jug along, and Clarence said, "How about havin' a little drink?"

And I said, "Okay."

Then all of a sudden he said, "Holy man! Look at there!" And honest t' gosh. I'll bet you that northern was as long as the gol damn door on my shack! I never seen anything like that. When I first looked at it, it looked like a fencepost. I know it was six or seven feet long!

I picked the bottle up. I said to Clarence, "Aw, hell, we don't want to spear them minnows!"

The boat kept passing along and we each took a drink out of that moonshine jug. Then I said to Clarence, "Turn this gol damn boat around and let's go back and see if that fella's still there."

We never saw him again. I'm sure if I'd have hit him he'd 'a throwed me in the lake. Because I'll bet you he weighed 35 or 40 pounds! That was in the bay, in the northeast corner of Nokay Lake, where the creek comes out of Eagle and into Nokay. We got all kinds of fish that night.

For a few years when I was a kid there was fishin' for market. It was legal all around here. All you needed was ice and barrels. You'd gut and gill the fish, pack 'em in ice, and haul 'em into town. From there they'd be shipped out. The people from Nokay, Portage, and other lakes around there hauled their fish to Brainerd.

The fish were caught on hook 'n line. They used spoon-hooks and cane poles, one pole on each side of the boat. And then they'd row, because there weren't any outboard motors then.

As a kid I sold fish to those commercial fishermen. I got 10 cents a pound for northerns. They sold mostly northerns from this area, but at certain times of the year they even sold crappies. I suppose they shipped those fish to the Twin Cities, or maybe somewhere out east.

Winter Spearing Days

Years ago I never knew anything about hook 'n line fishing in the winter time. It was always spearing. I did a lot of spearing through the ice on Portage Lake, between Garrison and Brainerd.

My dad and I batched over there one winter, on the north side. My grandpa, Conrad Isle, had a homestead there. I was sixteen years old, so it was 1914. I had a trapline for weasels and brush wolves. And we also had a fish house on the lake. One day my dad would be in the fish house, and I would run the traps. The next day I'd go in the fish house and he'd run the traps. We'd alternate.

We had a great big box, I suppose about 4 feet square. I chopped a hole in the ice and we put the box down in there. That was what we used as a refrigerator. We'd put the fish in there. That was just out from shore, right out from where we lived.

We never got any really big fish, but they were nice—maybe a four or five-pound average. About once a week I'd go to Brainerd with my uncle, when he'd go after supplies. I'd take a sack full of fish along and peddle 'em, so I'd get a few bucks. Everybody would buy a fish!

I remember one time I sold a good-sized northern, maybe 10 or 12 pounds. I speared that bugger, and he had a pound-and-a-half black bass stuck in his throat. The tail was stickin' out. I sold that northern to a guy who was a game warden at the time. For quite a while after that he'd joke about that fish. He'd tell me, "Charlie, you beat me on that one. That fish wasn't all northern!"

LeRoy Chiovitte

17-Pound 8-Ounce State Record Walleye From Sea Gull River, 1979

LeRoy Chiovitte made his record walleye catch on Sunday of opening weekend, May 13, 1979—a 17-1/2-pound trophy from the Sea Gull River, about a mile from where it enters the southeast corner of Lake Saganaga. A resident of Hermantown, LeRoy had been making annual opening weekend jaunts to that area with an old school friend, Lorin Palmer of Cloquet, and Palmer's son Todd.

Following is LeRoy Chiovitte's personal account of his record walleye catch.

On our opening weekend trips, Lorin Palmer and I fish Lake Saganaga or the Sea Gull River, depending on conditions. The progress of the spring makes a big difference up there. In most years you can get some small walleyes in the river, and every once in a while a few decent ones, but normally we'd be fishin' in the lake for opening. It's pretty unusual to have the conditions we had for the 1979 opener, with those big walleyes still in the river. Things were really late. Even so, of the 19 walleyes we caught the first two weekends, 17 were already spawned out—as late as the spring was.

I don't think Saganaga gets all that much fishing pressure, partly because it's not that easy to fish. It's a big lake, and during the spawning season the big fish are pretty well concentrated. So you've got to know what you're doing. Also, because of all that BWCA hassle about motors and other things, I think a lot of people who used to fish there just aren't goin' anymore.

Anyway, we left Duluth on Friday afternoon, the day before fishin' season. We picked up our minnows at Jim's Bait Shop in

Duluth. Lorin and I bought a little of everything—chubs, shiners, leeches, and dew worms. We got up there around 11 that night and moved into our cabin. This was at Gordy's Place on Gull Lake, which is really just a widening of the Sea Gull River. Gordy's a guide up there and he's got some cabins and boats. We used one of his Aluma-craft boats.

It wasn't long before we got out fishin'. Our lines were in the water at about 1 o'clock Saturday morning. There was still float ice along the shore, so we had to push through about 30 yards of that stuff before we got out to the open river. The fishing spot was about a mile downstream from our cabin.

Actually, we fished in the same place all weekend. It was a hole right at the head of a rapids. We'd just get out of the current a little and drop two anchors, one at each end of the boat. They held fine. We'd cast out into the current and drag back slowly toward the boat. I was using 8-pound test Maxima monofilament, that Chameleon line. We used just a plain bare hook with a split shot sinker. I used an Eagle Claw size four, bronze color. That's a fairly small hook, but I'd rather use a smaller one.

So we got down to that spot and fished all night until 8 or 8:30 Saturday morning. I think we got three walleyes before daylight. I know I didn't get any during the night. But at about 6:30 or 7 in the morning I caught a 12-1/2-pounder, a big spawned-out female.

Now over the years Lorin had been in the boat when four or five 12-pound walleyes were caught. But he had never caught one himself. He always said if he got one that big he'd have it mounted, so when I got my 12-1/2-pounder that morning he was after me about getting it mounted. I'm not a great nut about mounting fish, so I told him I'd fillet it and eat it. The only fish I'd ever mount, I told him, would be an 8-pound brook trout or a state record walleye! Little did we know what would happen later that weekend!

We had four walleyes, including my 12-1/2-pounder, when we went back to the cabin at 8 o'clock Saturday morning. We had a bite to eat, a cup of coffee, and took a nap. Then it was fishing again from 3:30 Saturday afternoon until 11 o'clock that night, with maybe a couple fish. But I didn't catch any on that run. I know we didn't have a bite for at least four hours before quitting that night. We stayed in that same spot because we figured it was as good as anywhere else. We had already caught fish there, and we had it pretty much to ourselves, although there were a few other people fishin' there. Some would come in there and then leave.

We knew that the fish were biting really light. A lot of times a

LeRoy Chiovitte with his 17-1/2-pound Minnesota record walleye.

guy would have a bite and not even know it, especially if you hadn't done much fishing. And we seemed to be catching as many fish as anybody, so there wasn't much sense in moving around. But there was one boat across the way from us—a guy and his kid who fished the first night and into Saturday—that had the best catch I remember. I think they had 11 walleyes from 7 to 11 pounds.

The river isn't very wide where we fished. You can cast across it easily. I remember the current was increasing and the river was rising all weekend. As a matter of fact, I started out with one fair-sized split shot but ended up with three of them, just to get the bait down. There's a rocky and gravelly bottom in there.

During the night you could hear the fish moving up the river. There's a deep channel through there, but otherwise the water's fairly shallow. So you could hear 'em splashin'. They seemed to move in spurts. To tell you the truth, I thought they were suckers because I had seen suckers splash around like that. I'd never seen walleyes do it. But I know they were walleyes because we got a look at a few of them. I don't think they were in the act of spawning, just lots of 'em moving in the river. We don't use lights while we fish, but we keep a flashlight handy in case we really need a light. We don't use it otherwise—and hope we don't get tangled up!

It was cold, always cold that weekend. The first night we had snow, but I think there was some sunshine by Sunday. I don't like to wear gloves when I'm fishing, but fingers got cold if you weren't busy. And we weren't that active. Saturday night things slowed down to a standstill. So we quit fishin' about 11 o'clock, with the idea that we might as well get some sleep while they weren't bitin'. Then we'd go back early in the morning. We wanted to make sure we'd get back into our spot.

We got down there at 3:30, early on Sunday morning. Todd wasn't along on this trip. He wasn't very optimistic after Saturday, so he decided to sleep in.

Now Lorin and I always have a little competition going, to see who can catch the most fish. When we went out early Sunday morning he had me down by two fish. We caught three fish Sunday morning and I caught 'em all, so I beat him in the end. I caught my last one around 8 o'clock, and that was the big one!

I had cast out as usual and was slowly working my line back toward the boat when it suddenly felt like I was comin' up on a snag. You could usually feel your sinker hit a rock and then you'd be snagged. That's what I thought I felt this time, but automatically dropped the rod tip, just in case it was a fish. I waited a few seconds and then I snapped 'er, like I was setting the hook. It didn't move so I figured for sure it was a snag. I snapped 'er again, and this time I knew I had a fish. It started swimmin' upstream!

The fish made four, five, or six runs upstream. It took line off my reel with no problems at all. I'd ease 'er back and then she'd go upstream again. They weren't big long runs, maybe only 20 or 30 feet, or maybe a little more. So the fighting wasn't all that spectacular. It was more of a heavy pull, no big thrashing around. But when it wanted to go someplace it moved. You could feel it had the power.

Now it drops off fast, maybe eight or 10 feet, into that hole we were fishin'. But our boat was anchored in shallower water, not far from shore. There was a guy fishin' in a boat just a little ways from us, and, as I worked the fish close to the boat, he saw it flash in the water. He hollered, "It looks like it's going around your anchor!"

I tried to stop it, but I couldn't. Sure enough, it's in the anchor rope. Lorin looked over the side, and down there was this big walleye with about two feet of line between him and the anchor rope.

He was looking at the rope, just fanning his tail, not struggling. So Lorin carefully reached down, got hold of the rope, and started to raise up the anchor. The fish still didn't fight. It came right up with the anchor and Lorin got it in the landing net. Meanwhile, I'm still sitting at the other end of the boat, holding my rod and wondering what's happening with my fish!

About the time Lorin lifted the net, the weight of the fish tore the hook out of its mouth. But he brought the fish into the boat, plus the anchor, the rope, and my line which was mixed in there, too. The fish didn't really bounce around much. Bob Adam and his boy, from Edina, were fishing near us and saw what happened. They knew Lorin, so they said, "Why don't you hold it up and we'll take a picture of it." They took the picture and the fish didn't struggle at all.

Now when I laid that big walleye down in the boat I wasn't thinking "state record." I was thinking of that St. Paul *Pioneer Press* fishing contest! I had entered that 12-1/2-pounder the day before, but as soon as we got it to End of the Trail Lodge for the weigh-in we found out that bigger walleyes had already been weighed. My fish was in the top four or five, but not really in the ball game. A guy just doesn't catch that many 12-pound walleyes, so I figured there went my last chance to win that big contest.

So the next day I get this bigger fish! When I lifted this walleye I knew it was quite a bit heavier than 12-1/2 pounds. Lorin's anchor was out already, so I pulled mine and said, "Let's go weigh it!" So we made another trip to End of the Trail Lodge, on a backwater of the river. I laid the fish down but did stick a stringer through its mouth and tied that to the boat. I didn't want it to flop around and get back in the water! But the thing never flopped its tail once. It was alive all the time but never jumped around until we had it sittin' on the scale. That scale had been certified in 1972. My fish registered 17 pounds 9 ounces on it. But when the scale was tested the next day they found it to weigh three-quarters of an ounce heavy, so the DNR listed it as 17 pounds 8 ounces. That was good enough for a top prize, a 7-1/2 horse Mercury outboard, in the St. Paul *Pioneer Press* contest. And it took over as Minnesota's state record walleye.

We knew where a bunch of game wardens were staying in the area, called them, and they sent somebody over to witness the fish. And that night I was on Butch Furtman's outdoors show on WDIO-TV, channel 10. I had known Butch for quite some time and thought he'd like to have the fish on his show. Naturally, he was quite interested. And as soon as I got off the show there was a DNR biologist there to examine the fish.

Gordon Morris, a good Duluth taxidermist, did a beautiful job on the fish. Gordy and I went to school together at Denfeld. Uptown Glass and Mirror, a company right near my house in Hermantown, built the glass case for the mount.

Pictures were taken up north and in Duluth. Now here's a good one. That Sunday afternoon, after we got back to town, we called the Duluth paper, thinking they'd be interested in taking pictures. This girl answers and says, "There's nobody here to talk to. Try calling back tomorrow morning."

We told her that if it's certified we'd have a state record walleye, and that the outdoor editor would surely be interested. But she said, "I suggest you call back tomorrow morning at 9 o'clock." I said, "Okay," and hung up.

A few seconds later the phone rings and somebody from the St. Paul *Pioneer Press* called up. He talked with me for quite a while, got the story, and said he'd like to have a picture of the fish. He suggested that I call the Duluth *News Tribune* and have a photographer come out. He said they could wire the pictures down to St. Paul. So I told him we had just called the Duluth paper and the gal told us to wait until the next morning. He couldn't believe it, so he put me on hold—I s'pose he made a phone call—and then he told me there'd be a photographer from the Duluth paper at my house in 20 minutes.

I caught the record fish on a good-sized shiner, a spottail shiner about four inches long. I've never tried artificials up there. It's always been minnows and some leeches, depending on time of year and conditions. We totalled 10 walleyes on that opening weekend of 1979, plus 9 on the second weekend, and only two bit on leeches.

And Lorin did get his 12-pounder, on that second weekend. He and Todd and I went back on Thursday night. We caught eight walleyes on Friday, one early Saturday morning, and then they were all done. This was the same place we fished on the opening.

I received a certificate from the State of Minnesota, showing that I had caught the record walleye. It's been quite an experience. A few times I've had guys make cracks about how they know "the real story," that the fish was snagged or whatever. At first I'd get angry, but then I began saying "the heck with it."

Three Department of Natural Resources personnel took part in the verification process. Some press accounts mistakenly reported that Grand Marais area fisheries manager Jim Storland witnessed the weigh-in. Actually, it was Keith Edman, conservation officer from Silver Bay, who went to End of the Trail Lodge for the weigh-in. DNR fisheries biologist Tracy Close of the French River Fisheries Headquarters examined the fish in Duluth. And Jim Storland checked out the scale used to officially weigh the new state record walleye. Following are their comments:

Keith Edman, Conservation Officer from Silver Bay, Minnesota
I was there when they weighed the record walleye at End of the Trail Lodge. I had been at Don Enzenauer's Voyageur Canoe Outfitters, another resort just a couple miles up the Trail. I just happened to be there when somebody from End of the Trail Lodge called up and asked for a conservation officer to come over and verify this big fish.

So I went over there. It was in the morning, probably around 10 o'clock. I saw the fish weighed. And they measured it for length and girth. I took down the names of the people who brought in the fish, and also wrote down the names of witnesses who saw the fish, both on the water and at the lodge. I sent this information to DNR Fisheries in St. Paul.

Tracy Close, Fisheries biologist at French River
I first saw the fish at WDIO-TV on Sunday night, right after LeRoy Chiovitte appeared with it on Butch Furtman's program. It was in the hall, just outside the studio. My wife was with me. Warren Kirsch, the regional fisheries manager, had called me up and told me to go to the studio. I just looked at the fish closely to make sure it wasn't snagged, and to verify that it was a walleye. That was it. I did no measuring or anything else there.

I did measure the fish later, at the taxidermist's office. It was in a cooler, not frozen. When they measured it earlier they ran the tape over the curve of the body and came up with something over 35 inches for length. But I measured it for straight-line length on a flat board, the proper way, and came up with a bit more than 33 inches, I think 33.3 inches.

I also took scale samples, pressed them, and examined them myself. I saw approximately 25 marks on a scale so I said it was probably 25 years old, or more. It was a good looking walleye! You know, quite often these big ones have lymphocystic growths or scars on them. But this one was in real good shape. By the time I saw it the fish had lost some weight. Eggs were running out of it.

From a Gunflint Trail lake? Hardly. These 11 walleyes weighing 74 pounds came from Lake Minnewaska at Glenwood, 1918. (Minnesota Historical Society)

There were eggs in the plastic bag where they first stored it. Later it was transferred to a cooler.

Author's note: Very few experts would expect a walleye to bite at this "ripe" stage of the spawning season. Mr. Close agreed. "We kind of wondered about that, too, but there were plenty of witnesses." And, he might have added, breaking "rules" is characteristic of cagey walleyes!

Jim Storland, Area Fisheries Manager at Grand Marais, Minnesota

All I did was verify the scale. I never saw Chiovitte's fish. I was called by Fisheries in St. Paul—after the fish was caught and already at the taxidermist's in Duluth. They wanted to make sure the scale was correct.

So I went up to End of the Trail Lodge. But first I took an object about the weight of the fish and had it weighed on a state certified scale at the Grocery Market in Grand Marais. Their scales are certified and checked periodically, since they're used for retail sale. I put the same object on the scale at End of the Trail Lodge and found that it was off by an ounce. It weighed an ounce heavy.

It was a regular good retail type scale, a meat scale. It just hadn't been certified recently.

Al Maas, Leech Lake Muskie Hunter

Al Maas is a well-known Leech Lake muskie fisherman. His guiding on Leech dates back to the early 1960's. He started out heavy on walleyes, including a several-year stint as launch operator for Dick's Launch Service at Walker. Later, as an independent guide, he began specializing in muskie trips. Al is a firm believer in catch-and-release muskie fishing. His story-telling inevitably carries a "big fish" theme.

"The Biggest Muskie I Had Ever Seen"

This goes back to when I had never strung a big muskie. I had been talking to Dick Knapp, who was a good Leech Lake muskie fisherman from Walker. Dick told me about a big fish he had spotted up in Sucker Bay.

Right after that I happened to be fishing in Sucker Bay with a man—I don't remember his name—but he was about 60 to 65 years old. We were fishing and suddenly this big fish came up behind the boat. I had never seen anything like it. My knees buckled and I dropped to the seat shaking. But I had enough sense to throw a jug out to mark the spot. There was a wind blowing from the southeast.

I went back over the area and I told this guy that this was really some fish. He didn't believe it. So he didn't worry about it at all. But I was ready and actually waiting for the fish. I don't remember what bucktail I was using at the time, but there he came and just inhaled it! I set the hook and he stripped off probably 125 yards of line, non-stop, and came out of the water. Now, I've caught a lot of muskies since then, and I can now estimate this fish to have been in the 50-pound bracket.

When the fish came up alongside the boat for the first time, the guy I was with got so excited he dropped his rod. I had a styrofoam bucket full of lures. He stepped into that and had lures hooked all over his pants leg! Then he got the net and was ready to dip the fish. But he had the net full of lures, too, so we had to pick that clean while the fish ran out again. The second time the fish came back he hit the side of the boat and knocked the guy over!

The next time the fish came back up was after 45 minutes of trying to land him. (Another guy witnessing all this had a watch.) We finally got the fish's head into my big salmon net, but it wouldn't fit. We got the head in there but that wasn't enough. The fish began another run and caught somehow on the back of the boat. The line broke just above my steel leader!

That fish consistently came out of the water at about 10-minute intervals and tried to shake the lure. It was quite a sight to behold. I tried for that fish for the next two weeks, but didn't get him.

A Muskie "Double"

When my wife and I first started fishing muskies, we went downtown to buy two lures. I bought a big Pikie Minnow and she

Leech Lake muskie specialist, Al Maas of Walker, Minnesota.

picked up a little yellow Mepps. I said, "What are you gonna do with that little dinky thing?"

So we took off and went fishing. We started fishing and she got two on right away, but lost both of them. We continued on and I switched to a Mepps—a yellow Giant Killer. As soon as I changed baits I had a fish come up that I figured was about 20 pounds. So I told her something like "here it comes," and then I pulled my lure out. The fish immediately swung over to her bait, hit her lure, and she set the hook. Meanwhile, I had cast out again and as soon as my lure hit the water another muskie hit. We had two fish, in the neighborhood of 20 to 22 pounds, coming in at the same time!

That's fun and games when you try to keep two muskies apart. We got both fish into the boat. I was going to release mine, and in so doing, as I jumped across the seat to help my wife, I slipped and landed on my fish and killed it.

I've had two muskies on simultaneously before, but that was the first time we ever landed a "double."

Jake Cline, Hackensack Memories

Jake Cline operated Cline's Minnows on Highway #371 in Hackensack for 23 years, starting in the late 1940's. He had lived in the lake country all his life, but seldom fished until he built the bait shop. During his bait shop years Jake Cline fished a lot, establishing himself as one of the area's most successful and colorful anglers.

"It Paid To Stay Later"
Stony Lake Walleyes and Pleasant Lake Crappies

I remember a number of times when it paid to fish after most people quit. One time Arnold Shephard was with me. We both had businesses in Hackensack and we fished together for many years. I had Cline's Minnows and he had the Trading Post. There was many nights when we fished walleyes at Stony Lake.

On this one special night we weren't doin' too hot. It got to be around 9 o'clock, way after dark. So we thought we'd go home. Well, instead we made another trip around the bay. We were trolling with suckers. And I got a bite! It turned out to be a 9-pound walleye. Before that all we got was a few small ones. Of course, our "small ones" were pretty good-sized.

So we thought we wouldn't go home. It was about 10:30 but we were gonna fish again. And during that night we caught six more big walleyes between seven and eight pounds. We wound up staying until about 12 o'clock.

Now that was fishing pretty deep, 12 to 18 feet of water. Our sinkers weren't too big, but we could feel the bottom.

Who caught the most fish? Ha! That was kind of a nip 'n' tuck situation. With Shephard and me, if I happened to be a catchin' too many, he'd start whistlin'. If it was the other way around and he

48

was catchin' too many, I'd do somethin' too. But on that fishin' trip there wasn't a great deal of difference in our luck.

That must have been in the early '60's, in the fall. But we caught some big walleyes on those night trips every year. My biggest was 12 pounds, and I've had a number over ten pounds. I've got one of them mounted, but it's still in the tackle shop.

Another time it paid to stay late was in the winter. I was at Pleasant one night, all alone in the fish house. It was gettin' pretty late at night, way after dark, so I thought it was about time for me to go home. I had caught a few crappies, but nothing special.

But then down went my bobber. And things happened! I caught 15 big crappies in a row! The biggest weighed 3 lb. 2 oz. I had three of 'em over three pounds, and not any under 2-1/2 pounds! I caught those 15 crappies in less than an hour!

It was awfully cold, and when I threw 'em out of the fish house they froze. So I stacked 'em up in my arms and carried 'em to the pickup. When I got to town it was just about 10 o'clock. They were just getting ready to close up at the Chat 'n' Chew restaurant. I made a couple trips to the pickup and carried those crappies inside there to show 'em.

We throwed 'em on the floor there and they took pictures. And they sent some to the St. Paul paper. So my picture with those fish was in the Sunday paper! And they put one big one in a drippin' pan and covered it with nice clean water and froze it. They showed that one off.

Birch Lake Walleyes At Ten Before Seven

When I had the bait shop in Hackensack there weren't any guides there. But once in a while somebody'd ask me to take 'em out fishin'.

I remember one fall I fished a lot on Birch Lake. That's right in Hackensack. I had been catchin' walleyes. So this one lady from Backus comes in and says, "I heard you caught some walleyes out there in Birch Lake." I said I did. And she says, "You don't s'pose you'd catch time enough to take me out fishin', would ya?"

I said, "I'll take you fishin' if you go with me at the right time. You won't believe it, and a lot of people wouldn't believe it, and it's hard for me to believe it! But those fish don't bite until 10 minutes before 7 o'clock!"

So here she comes about 4 o'clock! "When are we goin' fishin'?" I

told her they won't bite before 10 to 7. Finally about half past six I said, "Let's go."

So we went down there. I had a boat there on Birch. And don't you know, at 10 minutes before 7 o'clock her bobber went down with a walleye on it! That story went to Iowa and all over. She said, "Don't tell me he doesn't know what time those fish bite!"

We got seven walleyes that night. After that she knew what time to go. And she came back and fished pret' near every evening for a while. And she caught walleyes.

Of course, I remember about that time some resort guy came over and he wanted to try it in the morning. So we did, and I think we caught six walleyes that weighed 21 pounds altogether.

I've had marvelous fishin' in that Hackensack country! I've seen 'em go way up north and get skunked! And some of the small ones they bring back! I told 'em, "We use that kind for bait around here!"

The Car Spring Trick

This was in the winter time, on Pleasant Lake. Shephard, this fishin' buddy of mine, had a friend who didn't care what he did.

He'd fish one line, two lines, or three or four. He'd use tip-ups outside while he stayed in the fish house.

This one time he was in the fish house with Shephard while I was fishin' outside. I had told Shephard ahead of time that I was gonna pull a joke on this guy. So he kept him busy in the fish house while I went to work.

I had a car spring. And the spring had a hole in the center of it. So I took one of his tip-up lines, a heavy line, and tied it to the car spring. Then I let it down into his fish hole.

Well, the guy saw that his line was down. He ran out there and started pullin'. And you know how that spring would pull in—heavy and off to the side. He hollered, "Shephard! Come out here! I've got a big one!"

Every time he pulled, that spring would go this way, then that way. Of course he never slacked up. He just pulled away. And when he got it toward the top, near the hole, he broke the line.

Old Shephard, he had the door to the canvas fish house open so he could watch this guy try to pull in that car spring. He saw it all. And he just roared. He said, "I thought you knew how to fish! Lose a big fish like that!"

We didn't tell this guy about the car spring until the next time he came up. And that burned him right up! He said, "I've been thinking about that big fish and the broken line every day!"

That was something. That guy didn't care how he fished, with all those lines and everything. And he caught some big fish on those tip-ups. He was quite a drinker, too.

Hank Kehborn, Gone Fishing

Hank Kehborn is a professional story teller. He became a syndicated outdoor columnist following his retirement as veteran writer and outdoor editor for the St. Paul *Dispatch* and *Pioneer Press* newspapers. For years his "It's the Limit" columns have featured the fishing exploits of others. In the stories here, however, Hank goes afield himself.

Stroking a Muskie's Belly

Somewhere in the 1950's I was fishing up at Lake of the Woods with Ed Shave, Stu Mann, and a couple guys from Warroad. One of them was Marvin Tutt and the other, appropriately, was a guy by the name of Bill Fish. They were two local guys who knew the lake.

We left Warroad and went across the lake to camp on an island overnight. Of course that night we had a little of the grape with us so we sat around, as fishermen do, having a few drinks and a little food. And the fish stories were really going.

Marvin Tutt told about an old Indian trick he knew—stroking muskies into the boat. And the longer he told the story the better it got, until none of us believed him. In fact, even the next morning we told him, "Boy, you tied into that grape pretty good last night, giving us the one about putting a muskie to sleep by rubbing its belly!" But he insisted it's true. He said he learned it from some Indians.

Well, we were on a muskie fishing expedition anyway, so we went out, and I was in a boat with Marvin. Stu Mann was in another boat with a camera. I believe Stu got this thing on film and showed it on his TV show, because a lot of people wouldn't believe this.

Anyway, we were out for about an hour when Marvin tied into a muskie that weighed about 39 or 40 pounds. He worked it up to the boat and said, "Now watch this!"

He leaned over, and, when he had this big muskie alongside the boat, he put his hands under its belly and began to stroke it. And would you believe that muskie went to sleep and he lifted it right out of the water. It didn't kick a bit!

Meanwhile I was at one end of the boat ready to bail out. Because I knew that a big muskie on the loose in a boat could kick around and take legs off. But Marv held it up and kept stroking it, and that muskie was perfectly still—petrified, like a log. He held it there for a few moments and then put it back in the water and said, "Now, Hank, you try it!" But no way was I going to try that.

The fish lived to see another day because we released it. Marv said to me, "The next one we get you'll have to stroke." But fortunately we never caught another muskie that day.

I had never heard of that belly stroking business before, but later I learned that it's popular among muskie fishing experts.

Hank Kehborn and Ed Shave Portage In
Yanking on Ed's New Outboard

I'll tell you another one about fishing the Lake of the Woods area. This one concerns Ed Shave. I went up there with Ed one time, just the two of us. The old-timers up there had filled us full of glory tales. You know how they go. You gotta hide behind a tree when baiting your hook because the muskies are so savage. And they all weigh 50 and 60 pounds!

Now Ed had a brand new outboard motor, still in its crate. It was a McCulloch, just like the chain saw. I don't think they made those motors too long. Anyway, we picked up the motor in St. Paul where they had an outlet. The idea was to have Ed, the famous outdoor writer, test this motor.

So we drove up to Warroad and loaded our stuff on a big launch that took us across the lake to the Canadian side. We had a map and Ed knew where to go. Our plan was to portage in to this lake where muskies the size of two boats were supposed to be lurking all over. It was one of those lakes which "nobody fishes" and which "nobody knows about."

We broke this motor out of its crate, got everything ready, and began to portage in to this lake. It was about a mile, or a mile and a quarter, over deadheads and through brush. Now a 5-1/2 horse motor isn't all that heavy, but it's damned awkward carrying it on your shoulders, toting other gear, and crawling through the woods. And it was a terribly hot day, just a miserable day!

But we made it in to the lake and found a boat there, like we were told. We put the rods and tackle boxes in the boat and shoved off. I got behind the oars and rowed us out a ways. Meanwhile Ed put the motor on, tightened it down, and started yanking. And, boy, he really yanked away. But it wouldn't start!

I was hollering about getting hump-backed from rowing the boat. And Ed was swearing while he yanked and yanked. He took the top off the motor and fooled around, then put it back on. He did everything possible and kept yanking on that starter cord.

I'm still rowing and I said, "Well, Ed, how much longer is this going to take?"

In kind of a low voice he grumbled, "Not very long."

Then he unscrewed the clamps that held the motor to the boat. And I thought he was gonna bring it into the boat and really work on it. But instead he picked it up and tossed it in the lake! And this was the first time that motor had been on a boat. A brand new motor! Ed said, "I'll be damned if I'm gonna carry this thing back through those woods again."

We wound up rowin' around that damn lake and didn't catch a fish all day. And all I could think of was that brand new motor down on the bottom.

Charlie Lembke's Secret Bass Lake

There was an old-timer up at Big Fork by the name of Charlie Lembke. He was from Chicago and owned a ma-and-pa type resort on Owen Lake. Charlie was an old-time athlete who played football with George Halas and against George Halas in the days of the Canton Bulldogs. That was years and years ago.

Charlie wasn't a very big guy. But he was a helluva bass fisherman. He lived for bass, and he knew some good bass lakes where I used to go with him. Every time I got up in that area I'd try to get out fishin' with Charlie.

So this one time I'm up there with my wife Kathrine and our two kids, Jim and Linda. Charlie wanted me to go with him to some special lake. Well, here I was involved in this secret lake business again. It seems one of them is like the other. It's so virgin nobody's on it. Nobody even knows it's there. It doesn't have a name. Unless you know how to get there you'll never find it. And this one, according to Charlie, was "loaded with bass."

Here again, I'm lugging gear into a magical hotspot. This time we took a boat and a motor. We dragged that boat over the deadheads and around the stumps, and we carried the motor and the tackle for a good three-quarters of a mile. The deer flies just about ate us alive. And it was unbearably hot. It had to be 100. But we got in there and I looked at the lake. I thought to myself, "Gee, Charlie's right. There isn't a soul on this lake."

Of course, after the fishing trip I understood why nobody was

there. We fished that lake all day long and didn't catch a bass. Not one! And we fished it hard in that heat. We even got blisters from the sun and our lips were parched.

Now get this. We arrive back at the cabin and here Kathrine is frying potatoes—and bass. There were the most beautiful bass, all filleted. I looked at all this and said to her, "Where in the hell did you get all those fish? I damn near killed myself all day with Charlie and got nothing!"

She told me the kids caught 'em, down on the dock in front of the cabin. And you know what they were using for bait? They caught that beautiful stringer of largemouth bass on bubblegum, pink bubblegum! We had 'em for supper and they were great.

I tried bubblegum afterwards with no success. But for the kids it worked.

You know, that Owen Lake where we stayed was a good bass lake. But for some reason Charlie said this other one was better. It seems you gotta go lookin' for those hot lakes and they wind up killing you in the end!

Harlow Ellsworth, Hawg Hunter

Harlow Ellsworth has a reputation for catching big largemouth bass. Rarely going beyond a 50-mile radius of his home in Park Rapids, Ellsworth made a name for himself by concentrating on big bass, "hawgs" over four pounds. He's no standard run-of-the-mill bass pro—using an oar for his "depth finder," tossing spinner-bait-plastic worm combinations a foot long, and hunting big bass in shallow bulrush cover. Unconventional as they are, his methods have worked for him. In the years 1974-77, for example, he boated 238 largemouths over four pounds, including 22 over six pounds and five 7-pounders!

Lunker Largemouth Bass

A Trail of Broken Rods

Whenever I hear about "tackle-busting action" I think of a trip to one of my pet lakes for big bass. I've caught quite a few of my 6 and 7 pounders from that lake, which I fish from point to point. I fish my way around the lake, stopping to cast at these hot spots

Anyway, I got started this one morning before daylight. Right away I got into a five pounder. At the next point I dropped my plug about 45 feet back in the weeds and all hell busted loose back in there. I had a good one!

I was fishing with 7 foot Heddon Brute Sticks at the time. I reared back and set the hook, and I snapped the Brute Stick I was using right at the reel seat! The rod dropped into the water and the reel fell into the boat. And here I am sitting there, holding a little stub of the handle. I reached down, scrambled around, and picked up the line and started hauling it in.

I hauled that bass out of 45 feet of bulrushes. And she was a rootin' and a squealin' every inch of the way. She'd want to tie a

knot around every clump of weeds, every piece of rush she'd come to. You know how bass are. They'll run their noses down through the heavy clumps, trying to hang the hook and shake away.

I wound up cutting my finger on the line—down to the bone—before I got her hauled out. About the time I got her out to open water, the wind was quartering the boat back into the weeds. So I had to hang onto the line with one hand while pulling on the oar with the other to get back into open water. During that time Mama Bass got the line back around my big motor! Now the bass was close to the boat, so you can imagine me trying to untangle the line from the motor and working the landing net at the same time.

Luckily, my spinnerbait was buried in the top of the fish's head. After considerable splashing around and maneuvering, I boated that hawg—a 6-lb. 14 oz. largemouth bass!

So I had two big bass and it was still early. I continued on and worked two other spots which didn't produce. Then, about quarter to seven, I got into this other good point and threw a plastic frog about 90 feet back into the rushes. All of a sudden—bang! I came up with a really good one. After seven or eight minutes of gruntin' and groanin' and pulling that fish through every thick piece of bulrush she could find, I got her right about to the edge. I stopped and put three or four strokes on the oars because, again, the wind was blowing me into the rushes.

And right as I got to the edge, in open water, there's about five little pieces of bulrush sittin' all by themselves. And my fish heads for them! I put the rod in my chest and I got the reel about two inches in front of my nose. I'm grinding away as fast as I can and she's taking line away from me.

Now I got a look at that bass, and I know she was 9, 9-1/2, or 10 pounds like nuthin'! I gave one little extra pull and pop went my second rod! I let the fish get into that clump of rushes, she hung the bait, and got away.

So here I sit, quarter to seven in the morning, with two big bass in the boat, two 7-foot Brute Sticks busted, and nothin' to fish with. And the fish were turned on! What the hell could I do but go home?

Ed Morey, Fish Peddler from Motley

Morey's is a well-known fish company based at Motley, Minnesota, 20 miles west of Brainerd on Highway #210. Ed Morey started the firm as a one-man fish peddling venture back in the 1930's. His business grew from a few boxes of fish to a multi-faceted buying-processing-sales operation involving millions of pounds and dozens of species. In 1979, the Minneapolis-based International Multifoods Corporation purchased Morey's Fish Company.

In Minnesota, a fishing guide might tell a complaining client, "If you want a guaranteed limit go to Morey's!" Many a limit has been "caught" over Morey's retail counters in Motley and Brainerd.

The Morey Fish Company
A History By Ed Morey Himself

Back in the 1930's there was a fisherman from Lake of the Woods who had a sister living in Motley. In the fall of 1937 he stopped to see her on his way to Minneapolis, where he planned on selling some fish. I guess he was having truck trouble.

Anyway, I walked into the garage there and he talked me into peddling his fish. I had been selling vegetables and Sunday papers, anything to make a living then. So I wound up trading him corn for those fish! I had to go out in the field and snap off the corn which I gave him for three boxes of fish from Lake of the Woods.

There were walleyes, perch, and saugers in those boxes. And then he pulled quite a deal on me, which I'll never forget. He had a couple cans of "catfish." I didn't know one fish from another at that time, so when he told me the cans were full of catfish I believed him. I took all the fish out and peddled 'em. And I sold those two cans of catfish to a meat market in Little Falls. Later on I found out the darn catfish was burbot—eelpout! But they didn't know the difference. They sold 'em and never complained. Some years later we had a big laugh over it.

That was my first experience with selling fish. After that I worked into the fish business gradually. I peddled fish around the countryside to individual stores, anyplace I could sell a fish, especially in Motley, Wadena, Clarissa-Browerville, Long Prairie, and Little Falls to begin with. Then I widened out, carrying fish as far to the southwest as Morris and Montevideo. I'd make a trip to Montevideo in a day and peddle along the way. I was all alone.

These were fresh and frozen fish, mainly frozen. I had been buying a few fish from Lake of the Woods, but then I found out about the fish companies in Duluth. I started buying fish up there, including some smoked fish.

About this time I got the idea that smoked fish might be a good deal. I had seen a few smoked fish in the stores, here and there, but not many. I figured there might be a profit in it. So I had some fish smoked at a meat market in Clarissa, northerns and tullibees. And I sold 'em.

I was experimenting on my own at the same time. I was still buying smoked fish from Sam Johnson and learning about smoking from him. In the fall of 1938 I built a small 4' x 6' smokehouse on a little farm near Motley. My first attempt at smoking involved some tullibees from Lakes of the Woods. Out of that first batch I lost every single fish! Right into the fire! But after that I learned fast.

Before 1940 I bought all kinds of fish from Sam Johnson in Duluth—northerns, walleyes, lake trout, herring, ciscoes, and all kinds of smoked fish. He got his walleyes from Canada and served as kind of a middleman between me and his sources. Finally I got enough volume so I could buy direct from Canada. I'd buy fish out of Winnipeg that came from all over Canada. They produced fish in winter when I needed them for smoking, while Lake of the Woods fisheries operated only from June 1 to November 1.

Of course I didn't operate through the summer months until 1940, when I built my first retail fish house and a smokehouse in Motley. That's when I began buying a lot of fish at Lake of the Woods, shipping, and getting more and more into an active fish business. That first smokehouse was a wooden building with wooden smokers on the side. We got by there and smoked a lot of fish! And we started to get some bigger accounts.

My first big account, obtained in 1940, was the National Tea Co. I can still remember when they ordered 10,000 pounds of smoked whitefish, all in one order. Now you know it takes a lot of work, a lot of smokin', and a lot of fish for 10,000 pounds of smoked fish! I guess it took me three or four days, with a lot of help. But we filled that order, which was our biggest up to that time. Later on, with bigger and better facilities, it would have been routine.

For seven seasons after 1940 I operated a fresh-fish buying station on Lake of the Woods, located on Wheeler's Point at the mouth of the Rainy River near Baudette. I took over facilities from a private party, but the Booth fish company had operated there at one time.

I'd buy fresh fish from Lake of the Woods commercial fishermen and sell them on the fresh-fish wholesale market. The fish were shipped out in railway ice cars. We made the railroad connection in Warroad. We'd ship fish to Milwaukee, Chicago, Atlanta, Philadelphia, and all over. At our buying station we did only rough processing—gutting and gilling if necessary, but mainly packing 'em round, in ice. We'd run from June 1 to November 1. In winter I'd start smoking again.

In 1947 my first place of business burned down. The new fish shop we built to replace it was closer to town. The new place had refrigeration facilities which I didn't have before. Before that I

Ed Morey, the famous fish peddler from Motley.

had to depend on commercial refrigeration. At this time, with our new plant, we began year-round operations. Over the years I expanded, and we became one of the largest fish smokers, volume-wise, in the United States. We became unique with the many facets of our business. We process our cut fillets from fresh and frozen fish that come in here. We process the fish, sell the fish, and smoke fish. We have a jobber's business, a wholesale business, and retail stores in Motley and Brainerd.

As Morey's Fish Company grew we needed more fish. I'd buy fish from Lake of the Woods, Canada, and all over. As I expanded our filleting operation at Motley, along with the smoker, we needed lots of fish—millions of pounds! Back in the 1940's I bought a few fish from the Indian fishing cooperative at Red Lake. Through the 1960's and 1970's we were buying increasing amounts of fish from Red Lake, as well as fish from all over Canada through Canadian Fisheries at Winnipeg.

In 1970 Morey's bought out Selvog Fisheries of Warroad, Minnesota on Lake of the Woods, and we operate a fish buying station there. We have a manager and workers, who take fish in from Lake of the Woods commercial fishermen. They sort 'em and pack 'em in ice. We also have a truck that goes around to the Canadian side of Lake of the Woods, picks up fish, and brings 'em back to Warroad.

The fish we get from Lake of the Woods and Red Lake are trucked fresh, on ice, to our Motley processing plant. Other fish we get, from Canada, Alaska, or wherever, are brought to us frozen. That includes, for example, our lake trout and the smaller smoking whitefish, most of which come from Great Slave Lake. I've been going to Alaska since 1945 and have plenty of connections up there, especially for salmon.

You can imagine how fish prices have changed over the years. The first walleyes I bought from Lake of the Woods cost me 5 cents a pound. In 1978 we paid as high as $1.05 per pound for Lake of the Woods walleyes in the round, right out of the water, before any processing! When a semi backed up to our door at Motley in 1978, his load of fresh walleyes on ice was worth 25 to 30,000 dollars, depending on how many fish he had. That was before we touched 'em! A truckload of walleye fillets going out of here was worth about 100,000 dollars! And things weren't getting cheaper.

I told you that in 1940 we scrambled to fill an order for 10,000 pounds of smoked whitefish. To show you how we grew over the years, look at these orders. One restaurant operator from Ohio, with several restaurants, ordered 150,000 pounds of a certain sized walleye fillet. That's one customer, one order, in 1978. That fall we bought 45,000 pounds of king salmon from Alaska to smoke and steak for our own retail stores in Motley and Brainerd.

Ed Morey's Short Stories

One time four fellas came in to our Motley store. They had been up north spearing some place. And they really got skunked. In fact, I don't think they ever got into a fish house!

But they came in here, and they wanted four or five of the biggest northerns we had. Well, it just happened that I had saved some from that previous fall. They had the heads on 'em yet but the insides were out. They took those fish and, believe it or not, they tried to run a spear into those frozen northerns so it would look like they speared 'em! That was right inside the fish shop.

Then they took 'em outside, took pictures of 'em, and then they took 'em home. Those northerns were from Lake of the Woods and they weighed about 20 pounds apiece.

From about the middle of September into about the middle of October, the northerns run fairly heavy in the commercial fishermen's nets. So we usually have quite a few northerns around at that time. One day a fella drove in here, to our Motley store, with a camper. He wanted a big northern. You see, he was after a picture of himself with a big northern. So we found him one, maybe 15 to 20 pounds.

He took it outside, stood in front of his camper, had the picture taken, paid for the fish, and went home! We get quite a few of 'em like that.

Lots of times we've had fellas come in here to buy fish after getting skunked up north. They didn't want to lie a hundred percent about getting fish. So they'd buy their fish and then ask us to throw 'em to them over the counter! That way they could go home and say they caught 'em.

They'll joke about "catching" fish that way. They say, "See? We caught that fish!"

Torsk is simply a Norwegian name for cod. But a lot of people don't know that. One time I got a call from Minnesota's commissioner of agriculture. He said that a woman was raising thunder

A joke among Minnesota anglers: "If you want a guaranteed limit, go to Morey's!"

with some store for selling her cod for torsk. He asked me for the story on torsk.

He said, "What in Sam Hell is torsk? She's causing so much trouble over it, but I don't know what torsk is!"

So we explained that torsk is a Norwegian name for cod. The store guy wasn't doing anything wrong. It's all the same fish. But she thought she was being swindled, getting cod for torsk.

Considering the thousands of fish we've processed, I've seen very few deformed ones. But one time we found a northern with a horn on his head. It was a bony structure that stuck up about an inch, just behind his eyes on top of the head. It was a five or six-pound northern from Lake of the Woods.

For three or four years back in the early 1950's we'd buy one or two semi loads of big walleyes from Lake Erie. They'd only run a short time in the spring, in May.

We'd buy them in 100-pound boxes. The average was about 10 walleyes to a box. Yes, there were a lot of 10-pounders! I had 'em seven fish to a box, too! We'd pay 10 cents a pound for those walleyes in the round, cheaper than fish from Lake of the Woods.

The fillets off those fish were huge, very thick. We'd cut 'em up into serving size pieces. We'd fillet 'em and cut the fillets cross-ways.

The biggest one I know of weighed 18 pounds with the insides out!

Stories From Veteran Fly-in Pilots

In 1946, following Air Force duty in Europe, Don Hanson began a long career of flying fishermen into the lake country north of Warroad, and also carrying mail between Warroad and points in the Northwest Angle area of Lake of the Woods. He operated Hanson Airways until 1974 when he sold out to Fuzz LePage, who also took over the flying business of the late Maynard "Swede" Carlson. At one time the legendary Swede flew for Hanson Airways. When I chatted with Don Hanson in late 1979 he was still flying for Fuzz LePage's Warroad Airways.

Ernie Hautala, known as "Hoot" in the Ely area, helped pioneer bush flying in Minnesota's Arrowhead region. "He's one pilot we'll never forget," one Ely native told me. "If you were camped out in the wilderness on a dark stormy night and heard a lone plane go over, you could bet it was Hoot!"

Though long retired when I met him, Hoot tells of his adventures with unusual and exciting vividness.

Ernie Hautala of Ely

Dusty Rhodes, a B-5 Ryan, and Hoot
Gets Off the Ground

I bought a plane and started my flying business in 1932. Before that, in the 1920's, I got some flying experience from Dusty Rhodes of Tower. Cecil was his name but everybody called him Dusty. He used to fly around these north woods years ago. He must have been of World War I vintage.

Dusty had a plane that was similar to Lindbergh's. A fella from Eveleth, a mining man, put up the money for it, a B-5 Ryan. Of course, Lindbergh's was a little different because it was set up for

67

going across the ocean. Dusty's had a bigger engine. You needed that power for pontoons, to get out of these lakes.

Dusty had a hangar right on the bay of Lake Vermilion that you see from the highway before you get to Tower. And I used to help him there—gassin' up and other work. Dusty was a good operator. He was sober and industrious. And he worked like a horse. There was a lot of fur business at that time, a lot of trappers. So he was taking care of fur in this country, and in Canada, too. Hell, there was nobody on the other side of the border to watch it. There were no roads. Nothing but a big wide open space of emptiness! No people except for trappers.

When I started with my own plane I picked up a little passenger business, and this and that. I was kind of striving for a fishing business. I could see an opening there. We had a big wide open country that nobody was using, except for a few trappers. But it was a tough business at first.

Around 1938 or 1939 more and more people started looking to the airplane for getting back into the woods. They started to fly if they had the opportunity. People had been getting back in there, but with canoes and boats. And during the war, around 1940-41, a lot of 'em would have only a couple or three days, like a Saturday-Sunday-Monday. They wanted to make a fast trip. They wanted to go someplace quick, without spending a day to go in and a day to come out! Why, some of 'em had their rods and reels all ready when they stepped out of the airplanes! They'd have a bait in the water before the plane was unloaded!

So I got in a lot of flying time, sometimes 18 hours a day! I was going every day. I got so I could handle myself in just about any weather, daytime or nighttime. And that came in handy, because if you work a heavy schedule you've got to be able to cope with things. You couldn't just let a day go and have people pile up on you.

And there got to be a lot of people! There were fishermen, resorts starting up, people building cabins. And once this stuff got promoted we were loaded to the gills all the time. We put a few boats here and there on the lakes to take care of the overflow. If places were full you could dump 'em on a lake and they'd take care of themselves, camping out there for a day or two.

I didn't get involved too much with canoe outfitters. Oh, once in awhile I'd fly a couple fishermen in with a canoe, and they'd get back themselves. Or they'd canoe in and I'd fly 'em back. But I didn't want to be dragging canoes all over the place. I figured if a

A young Ernie Hautala c. 1940 next to his Stinson. "A bush pilot has to be sharp!"

guy wanted to go by canoe he could paddle the darn thing, for crying out loud!

Hoot's Longest Fly-in Trip

I flew from one part of the country to the other on different trips—Hartford, Chicago, Denver, down to Arizona, and all over. But on the bush trips up here the farthest I went was about 250 miles into Canada. You see, when I was in the flying business you could fly into the lakes north of Ely. But they closed 'em up in 1953, from the Vermilion River all the way to Gunflint Lake and Big Saganaga.

But that long trip into Canada. That was a good one! A couple of doctors from Chicago wanted to go up there for a week or two of fishin'. It was a crazy deal. This one doctor called me up and asked if I could fly them into a lake. What the hell was the name of that lake? We have one down here with the same doggone name. So I said, "Sure I can take you there." What the hell was a few miles?

So he sent me a telegram to substantiate the deal. They got to Ely all right and he pulled out this map. I said, "Hell. That's Canada!"

"Yah," he says, "That's where the lake is."

Well, that threw me all out of gear! I hadn't figured for all the time it would take for me to go up there and back. It threw everything out of schedule. But I had told 'em I'd take 'em, so I went up there. I took four or five cans of extra gas.

There was one building on that lake. The walls were full of holes, so even the mosquitos didn't know the building was there when they were flyin' around! But the way these guys were talkin' about the place it was really a big thing!

There was just an old fella up there—by geez, you know—an old trapper sittin' up there on that lake. And he had a couple of old flat bottom scows he had made. He was living in this old shack. And those doctors from Chicago thought he had a helluva place!

But they were happy. They had some friends up there, too. I don't know how they all crowded into that shack. And I don't know how they ever got back.

Anecdotes From Hoot

There was a guy selling fishing baits in Ely. It was in a store with a big long counter. There were baits all over the place. And this one fella who came in there was walkin' back and forth, up and down along the counter. He was lookin' at all these baits.

Finally the salesman said, "Say, here's a nice bait—right here!"

He just wanted to cut down on the time and get the guy out of there. This guy kind of looked at him and said, "Boy, I don't know. I don't like the looks of that."

Then the salesman asked him, "Who ya' buyin' that for? Yourself or the fish?"

One year, the first two fishermen I flew out in spring drowned! It was the latest spring I had seen, the latest ice-out, around May 25. That was around 1947 or 1948, somewhere in there. That year there was a lot of snow, and a lot of rain. The lakes were up four or five feet above normal. Water was pouring in everywhere.

Just exactly what happened to those fellas I don't know. It was a good-sized lake, and they were camping on an island. Somehow they tipped over with their canoe and drowned.

But boy! Were they eager to get up there! They wanted to go. It was one of those funny things. They had to get there in a hurry. And then they wind up like that.

The sheriff's department got in on it. And I remember we found the first one right away. But it took 30 days to recover the other guy. He had drifted off into a bay.

One time there were a couple fellas up at Ogishki Munchki, or something like that. It was a little lake with an Indian name, east of Ely. They were fishin', and they were gettin' smaller lake trout in there, about five or six pounds. Nice looking trout, though. They were bringin' 'em up pretty fast.

They had a chain stringer with the snaps. Each time they got a fish this one guy would put it on one of those hooks. And the other guy—I don't know why he did it—would take the whole chain off the boat each time his partner snapped on a fish. It was a crazy habit. And I was watching the operation.

Pretty soon they had their limit on there. And somehow or other, when the one guy threw the fish over the side, the other guy let go of the stringer at the same time. Those lake trout just kept going down to the bottom! The limit was five or six at that time.

And gee, you know. Those two guys were ready to jump in the lake! Ooh, they felt sad! So I told 'em, "What's the difference? Go ahead and catch some more. You've got another stringer."

By god, they got another limit of lake trout!

You know, on fly-in fishing trips everybody wants a place by themselves, where there's nobody else. This is the big thing. Everybody's got that idea in his mind—that there's the biggest fish in the world lurking down there, and he's the guy that's gonna catch it!

It's a good thing, too. They wouldn't go fishing without that anticipation.

Warroad's Don Hanson

Duck Soup at Sandy Beach

Any bush pilot who has flown nearly every day for many years has been stranded away from home. I've had it happen more than once, mainly when I was alone, but sometimes with people along. One time I had several people with me when I broke down up at Sandy Beach, out where the Selvog people fished commercially. All that was there was a commercial fishing camp, which included a cabin, a boat, and some other gear. I think the guys I flew in there were friends of the fisheries people.

Well, I dropped these people off and got into the plane for take-off. The wind was blowing pretty hard, from shore, so the lake was

calm on that side. I taxied out some distance and just as I was about to lift off the water I looked down and noticed an oil slick on the lake surface. I knew that meant trouble. As I remember that plane, the oil pump was somehow connected with the fuel pump, and there was a membrane of some kind that broke—so oil was pumping right out of the engine and onto the lake! I think that's how it worked. At least it was a poor arrangement.

I was out quite a ways already when I saw the oil and turned back toward shore. By the time I got close to shore the oil pressure went bad so I shut the engine down. The others had been watching, so they got in a boat and picked me up. I tried to overhaul this doggone oil pump business but it got dark on us. So I tied the plane down and we kind of got situated there for the evening.

Now, Sandy Beach is on the north shore of the big part of Lake of the Woods. When the wind's in the south you get its full blast there. I had told these guys that if the wind should switch into that direction, and the waves start coming in, we'd have to take the plane out of the water. The fisheries people had a winch down by the lake which they used occasionally for pulling boats out of the water.

Sure enough, the wind switched during the night and the breakers started rolling in there, so we winched the plane up on the shore. And there she blew—for two days! Now here's the clincher. The guys I flew in there forgot their groceries. All they had was a can of beans and a can of corn, or something like that. So I told 'em we better find something to eat. It was blowing like a son-of-a-gun.

I put on my hip boots, took my shotgun, and went back in the bog out behind there and I shot six mallards. It was blowin' so hard you could walk right up on 'em. It was nice hunting in that respect, but the walking was tough. It was back in there far enough so I had a good work-out.

One of the fellas in the party was their "cook," so I brought the ducks to him and told him we better have something to eat. We cleaned them and he made duck soup. This was a new one for me! I had heard about duck soup but had never eaten it. He had that can of corn and a couple onions, and maybe something else. Not much else, though. He boiled it all together, the mallards and the other ingredients, and I thought it was about the best thing I had ever eaten. Of course, all I had was coffee for the past 24 hours, so I was ready for something to eat!

I got the plane patched up and after a couple days the wind went down, so I got out of there. That was in the fall of the year, around 1952. The mallards were in nice shape, and I think they were in season. That wouldn't have made much difference anyway because we had to eat!

Big Walleyes on the Ice at 17-mile Reef

When I had my own flying business I didn't really go big on ice fishing. I just flew a few people into ice fishing spots and occasionally went fishing with them. This was before any amount of ice fishing took place on Lake of the Woods. There weren't any fish houses. And I didn't often go in the cold winter weeks, but rather when things were warming up, like in February or early spring. It seemed like wherever you'd dig a hole you'd catch fish. This was all on Lake of the Woods, on the American side.

Swede Carlson is the man who really got Lake of the Woods ice fishing off the ground in the Warroad area, with heated fish houses and fly-in trips. That was probably back in the early 1960's. He had a couple big sleeper houses which we still use today. We put one off Oak Island that sleeps up to 8 or 10 people. There are heated fish houses out there, and we leave a snowcat for their use. Swede started all that. And he also began to fly fishermen into a number of reefs. That reef fishing can be spectacular.

Lake of the Woods is such a big lake and there are so many nice spots to fish. When you go out ice fishing you have the feeling you want to dash from one place to another to test them all. You'd like to be a dozen people at one time. When you think about it, it's pretty fantastic to pick one spot on that huge lake, cut holes in the ice, and start pulling out 6-pound walleyes! But that's what happened one time when some of us were exploring.

Fuzz LePage was along, and so was Stub Pagnac of Stephen, Minnesota. We went out in the morning, more or less on a prospecting trip. I flew us out to 17-mile reef. We had our landmarks and found it all right. There was nobody out there. It's not that big an area, really, maybe a quarter mile long. It comes up to about 7 feet and drops off into 30 feet on each side.

I don't remember what the others were using for bait, maybe jigs and minnows. I had on a Swedish Pimple with about a six-inch drop line coming off of it with a minnow.

This Stub Pagnac was standing 12 or 14 feet from me hauling in 4 to 7-pound walleyes while I was catching mainly perch and saugers! Every once in awhile, though, I'd hook a big fish which wouldn't come through the hole. My line broke more than once. I

74

finally caught some big ones, too. That was a fantastic day. We had
our limits of big walleyes and plenty of other fish, even northerns.

The Ice Fisherman With No Boots, Just Oxfords

In recent years our ice fishing business has been done almost
entirely by reservation, so we have time to warn folks about the
conditions they might expect. We can tell them what to wear. You
see, sometimes people are unprepared for the outdoors. I've seen
them come up here on ice fishing trips in January without good
boots and heavy clothing—dressed like they were crossing the
street to the supermarket.

I was really worried about this one guy who came up with a
party of ice fishermen. He was really gung-ho about the fishing
but all he had on his feet was a pair of black oxfords. And it was
cold, like 20-below! Now usually if it looks like they'll have trouble,
I throw 'em a pair of boots or an overcoat. But these guys seemed
like all was okay, and this guy was gonna tough it out.

When I dropped them off on the fishing grounds I noticed this
guy had trouble getting out of the plane. And I also observed that
he didn't even flinch when I accidentally bumped his leg. At any
rate, he was ready to put in his fishing time out on the ice, in that
rugged cold weather, with nothing but street shoes on his feet.

I had dropped them off in the morning and went back for them late in the afternoon. When I picked them up this guy was still wearing those skimpy oxfords. As it turned out he had been a tank commander, or something like that, in World War II and was hit by a land mine. He lost both legs and was later outfitted with artificial legs. I guess he could feel no pain in those legs!

An Overturned Boat and a Mexican Strawhat
Trouble on the Way to Oak Island

In my years of flying over Lake of the Woods I've seen lots of fishermen in trouble—in boats during summer, and in snowcats and even 4-wheel drive vehicles in winter. I remember this one instance very well. It was in summer during a stretch when I was doing a lot of flying.

I was just getting ready to pull out of our base at Warroad early one morning. It was calm here, the wind being out of the southwest. About that time a group drove up to the landing here with two cars and two trailers with boats. They looked like fairly good lake boats but they had big motors on them. The rigs looked new.

So these two boats started out from Warroad and headed across the lake on their way to Oak Island. When they got out about 10 miles I could see this one boat was starting to have trouble. You see, I was watching them as I'd fly back and forth. Finally on one of my trips I spotted this one boat upside down with one of those big Mexican-type strawhats floating on the water. It looked pretty bad!

I flew on a bit farther and there, near Driftwood Point, was a boat going along with a lot of people in it. It looked overloaded to me. And they were waving this red jacket which I thought meant the worst—D-saster.

It was too rough for me to land, so I had to wait for news from Oak Island to find out what happened. As it turned out, they had been having engine trouble. And the farther they got out the rougher it got with that southwest wind. They had gone to the back of the boat to work on the engine, that big engine, and water came up over the transom. So when that group got swamped they shifted into the other boat. They made it safely to Oak Island, but that overturned boat and the Mexican hat bobbing on the waves had me wondering for awhile.

76

Leo Manthei, Blackduck Warden

Originally from Columbia Heights, Leo Manthei moved to Blackduck in July, 1949, on his first permanent assignment as game
warden. "When I started out," he recalls, "it was snowshoes, no
uniforms, no ties, no radios, and very little book work."

In his 30 years as conservation officer in the Blackduck area,
Leo became an avid fisherman, well known as a colorful "local
veteran." His many outdoor experiences included guiding important people on fishing trips—the likes of governors Orville Freeman and Karl Rolvaag.

Largest Sheepshead From a Minnesota Lake?

There were four of us in the boat—my wife Ann, our daughter
Eileen, and her husband Elmer. I was running the motor. It was in
May, 1968, right after the fishing season opened. We were fishing
for walleyes on Blackduck Lake, about an hour before sunset. We
had three or four walleyes on the stringer. And then my daughter
hooked something solid. We thought she was snagged.

Eileen was using an old Zebco outfit, with old 8 lb. test line that
probably hadn't been used for eight years! I figured it was an old
rotten line, so I told my wife to grab it and break it off. It was
windy and I was having a heck of a time handling the boat.

She grabbed the line and started pulling on it. Then she said,
"Leo, I think it feels like a fish!" I said, "Naw!" But she said, "It
does!"

So I told her to give me the line. I still had one hand on the
motor. I pulled on Eileen's line and I knew right away it was a
fish. And I knew it was a big one. Right away I'm thinkin' of a big
walleye!

I was running the boat and trying to land this fish at the same
time. It took a long, long time, because the fish stayed down there.

I said it had to be something in that 10 pound-plus class. And when I talked like that they started to work me over. "Don't lose it! Don't lose it, whatever you do!"

Finally I got to see it, a few feet down there. It kind of rolled and I thought for sure we had a walleye over 16 pounds! Now they were really yellin'. The next time I got him up he was a little closer and I saw his back. I said, "It's gonna go 20 pounds!" And I kept on thinking it was a big walleye.

But about the third or fourth time it came up it broke the surface with its tail. I got a look at that reddish tail. Then I knew what we had! I told 'em it was a sheepshead, and for a moment there I almost grabbed the line to break it off—in disgust! But my daughter wanted it so darn bad. And it was a big fish.

So when we got him near the boat I told Elmer, my son-in-law, to get ready to stick his hand into the fish's mouth, and to get a hold of the gill cover. They don't have teeth, you know. So he got a hold of it that way and we lifted him in. Once we got it in the boat it kicked around a lot.

The sheepshead is a good fighter. They'll stay down near the bottom, like a walleye. It took considerable time to get this one up. I

Leo Manthei's daughter, Eileen, with 26-lb. sheepshead from Blackduck Lake. Biggest ever from a Minnesota lake?

took it very easy. It was blowing hard and I had to fight that wind, trying to keep the boat near the fish. So I probably didn't experience his fight in the usual way. He stayed down, in about 12 feet of water. He just kept hangin' on the bottom down there, for a long time. He'd run, though. He'd stop, then go the other way again. But it was heavy, more like a big walleye than a northern.

It was dark, but Preston Anderson, the postmaster, came over to the post office to weigh the fish for us. I wanted an accurate weight. Then I gave the fish to Orin Wolden so he could have it mounted.

That sheepshead weighed 26 lb. 12 oz. I had taken a picture of a 16 lb. sheepshead from Blackduck Lake years ago. I thought that one was enormous. Sheepshead are common enough in Blackduck Lake, but I never thought I'd see a 26-pounder.

My daughter hooked the fish on a 3/8-ounce jig, one of my homemade jigs with no paint, and no tail material. Just the lead-head and hook. We were using them with rainbow minnows.

"I-s T-h-a-t Y-o-u, L-e-o?"

I've seen poachers so intent on their spearing that they don't know the warden is there—standing next to them with a hand on their gunny sack!

Orin Wolden is quite a man for fishing. He runs a contest out of his Union 76 station at Blackduck. He's got all kinds of fish mounts there. And he likes to tell the story of when I was lying under a cedar tree on the North Turtle River, waiting for spearers.

I had been parking in this one guy's yard for a few nights during a big walleye run. But no spearers showed up. So this one night I parked about a quarter of a mile down the road. From there I walked down to the river, and there they were—somebody spearing walleyes. I quietly crawled under this cedar tree near the river.

This one fella speared a walleye, and came up to the cedar tree to shake the fish off the spear. He was shakin' it back and forth right in my face! I was afraid I'd get stabbed, so I grabbed his spear.

This guy talks very slowly. He tells lots of stories with that slow voice of his. I recognized it right away. When I got hold of his spear, he said, "I-s t-h-a-t y-o-u, L-e-o?"

I said, "Yeh. It's me."

And he said, "O-h n-o!"

G. H. Nelson

Gustav Herman Nelson may sound like a herring fisherman's name. But this particular Scandinavian fisherman went for bigger Lake Superior fish, the mighty lake trout. Nelson's finest hour involved a lengthy battle with a huge lake trout which became recognized as a Minnesota record.

Jim Peterson reported Nelson's Memorial Day catch in the *Minneapolis Tribune* a couple days later, on Wednesday, June 1, 1955. Jim reported that lake trout had been hitting off Hovland. In addition to Nelson's big one, Lewis T. Bostwich of St. Paul had landed a 33 lb. 14 oz. laker in the same area.

Nelson's picture with his trophy lake trout appeared in the *Duluth News-Tribune* on the same Wednesday. An accompanying report observed that the "whopper" measured 43-1/2 inches long and was 29-1/2 inches in girth. The paper stated that Nelson's fish, which "socked a Pearl Wobbler," weighed 47 pounds. Why is it listed as 43-1/2 pounds in the record books? Mr. Nelson himself explains this discrepancy in the following account of his memorable trip to the waters off Hovland.

Trolling Out of Hovland
A Record Lake Trout

A fella by the name of Mr. T. J. Clark and I sailed with his motor launch all the way from Duluth up to Hovland, Minnesota. That's when I got my biggest lake trout, on Memorial Day Weekend, 1955.

Clark used to be the general superintendent over the car shops in Duluth and Proctor. I was a railroad man, too, working for the Northern Pacific from back in the 1920's until I retired in 1964.

We left Duluth in Clark's 30-foot boat on Saturday, pretty early

80

in the morning. But we never got to Hovland that day. A heavy northeast wind came up. And by the time we got to Two Harbors it was so rough that we pulled into the iron ore dock there. That was around noon. Clark tied up the boat and we went home to Duluth by car.

The bad weather kept us off the lake until Sunday afternoon, about 4 o'clock. That's when we started out for Hovland again, in Clark's boat. We travelled all of Sunday night and got up to Hovland early Monday morning, maybe 7 o'clock. We docked there at Gust Berglund's and had breakfast in town. Then we went out fishing.

It was a very nice day, a nice sunny day. There was no wind at all. The lake was laying just like a mirror. In fact, Mr. Clark made the remark that he had never seen the fish bite very good when it was so calm. Not enough movement of the boat or something.

We fished with outriggers, one line on each outrigger. Then we had two lines in the center. I was using a braided monel line. You see, years ago, to start with, they used straight copper line. They weren't so good. But then they came out with braided steel line, monel. That doesn't kink up. It's more pliable. I used 45 lb. test braided monel line.

Clark had just finished his remark about the fish not biting when it's calm, and my big fish hit. It was on my outrigger. I had 500 or 600 feet of line out, with a big heavy lead sinker that I had made myself—about 3/4 of a pound—in order to get down deep.

The fish put up a good fight for quite a while, from three-quarters of an hour to an hour. But by the time we got the fish to the boat there wasn't much life in it. He had come up to the surface from such deep water, you know. We didn't have a big landing net, nothing for such a big fish. So we gaffed him. We got the gaff under his head, underneath, and lifted him up into the boat. Clark and I worked together.

We weren't out for more than an hour before I got my fish. It was the first one we got, and the only one. We took it back to Hovland and weighed it on the fishermen's scale at the dock. It weighed 47-1/2 pounds. Now that was on one of those big counter balanced scales that was used for weighing fish. They are pretty accurate, you know. This one belonged to commercial fishermen in Hovland, the first one you came to in Hovland. Berglund was his name. He was a good friend of Mr. Clark.

We then had to drive the fish to Grand Marais for official weighing. It was at a garage there, an official weigh-in place. We made it back to Duluth that same day, Monday. Then on Tuesday my son and I drove down to Corrie's sportsmen's store in downtown Minneapolis, right across from the Foshay Tower. The fish was weighed there again and they put it on display until Thursday. Then I was on Rollie Johnson's TV show with the fish!

I won a bunch of fishing equipment—a tackle box, rod and reel, baits, and so forth for that week. Then, for the season prize, I won a $325 electric stove. That was in the fall, after the season closed. The people with the largest fish in each category went down there for the prizes.

I won second prize in the *Field and Stream* contest, lake trout division, for that year. A fella from Idaho beat me by 9 ounces! But my fish was originally bigger. I got credit for 43-1/2 pounds, the official weight. But that weighing didn't take place until in the afternoon, hours after I got the fish, early in the morning. It weighed 47-1/2 pounds on Berglund's scale, when it was fresh.

Right away, and for the trip to Minneapolis, I had the fish packed in dry ice. They kept it on ice down there. And I had ice on it coming back up north. So the meat was just perfect. I took the fish to a taxidermist in Duluth, on 6th Avenue, and he got the skin off and gave us the meat. We still have the mounted fish, in my son's recreation room in Eau Claire.

That was quite a fishing trip! A lot of people looked at that lake trout! And a photographer from Grand Marais took pictures.

G. H. Nelson's record lake trout was weighed at the Midway service station in Grand Marais, a popular weigh-in station for years. Official weight there on May 30, 1955, the date of the catch, was 43 lb. 8 oz. The fish was entered in Corrie's Sportsman's Paradise Fish Contest in Minneapolis on June 2, 1955 and weighed 37 lb. 5 oz. at the time of entry. *Field & Stream* listed the fish at 43-1/2 pounds.

Gordon Yaeger, on Whitewater Trout

From the Rochester Post-Bulletin

The second largest trout ever recorded for the Whitewater Valley, weighing a whopping 13 pounds, 14 ounces, was landed Monday, July 29, 1974 by veteran trout angler Edward Krieger of Elba. Exceeded only by the 14-pound trout of record, caught by the

G. H. Nelson of Duluth with state record 43-lb. 8-oz. lake trout caught while trolling on Lake Superior out of Hovland on May 30, 1955.

legendary Black Bill in 1947. Krieger's big fish was hooked just below the old bridge at the Crystal Springs fish rearing station.

"1 was hollerin' and hollerin' for help," Krieger said, after getting a glimpse of the size of the fish he had hooked. At first, he said, he thought it was a big carp, and it was five minutes before he got it off the bottom.

After about 10 minutes, he attracted the attention of Carl Nelson of the fish rearing station, along with some others, and they came to help.

Krieger, who is 71 years old, walks with a cane, and has been a trout fisherman in the Elba area for 52 years, played his big fish carefully.

"Black Bill taught me to fish," he said, "and I kept remembering what he told me: 'Keep the rod up so it has plenty of whip!' And I did it just that way."

Krieger fought the fish for about 20 minutes before he got it close enough to net. The first effort failed as the big fish swirled away.

Patiently he worked it back, and finally got it in the net...which promptly broke off at the handle!

But Krieger was to get his big fish anyway, for his net helpers—

John Huber and Robert Jensen—grabbed the rim of the net and swooped the big brown up on the bank.

It was just in time, too, for the hook had started to straighten out, according to Nelson, who runs the Crystal Springs installation.

"I was real calm when I was playing the fish," Krieger said, "but when it was finally on the bank I was shaking all over!"

The fish he caught had been in the stream a long time, Nelson said, despite the fact it was caught at one of the most heavily-fished spots in the Whitewater.

Now for the final detail. What was it caught with? A wet or dry fly of exotic character, or some similar secret weapon? Not so, and the purists be hanged. Old Ed caught it on plain garden tackle—a nightcrawler.

Terry Fussy's Record Channel Cat, And Praising the Mississippi

I was born and raised in the neighborhood of the Lowry Avenue Bridge. A lot of kids in that neighborhood spent plenty of time at the river. I was just a little more avid than most of them. I'd be down there fishing almost every day.

I can honestly say that I have never gone home from the Mississippi River, at the Twin Cities, without catching fish. You might catch crappies, smallmouth bass, catfish, or carp. There are times when we slaughter the walleyes. Northern are caught there, and even muskies! I've caught just about everything possible on that river, including rainbow trout!

This one day, in February, 1975, I just happened to be down at the river messin' around for carp or catfish, or whatever I could catch—something to practice my taxidermy on. There's a power plant a bit upstream from where I fish, and that keeps the water open in winter.

Anyway, this was one of those days that looked good for going down to the river and horsing around for awhile. It was early in the morning. I was fishing off a dock. It wasn't long, so it was sort of like fishing from shore. I was kind of daydreaming and puttzing around on the shore, with my rod wedged in a brick on the dock. I hadn't been there very long.

I walked back up to my rod, And all of a sudden it just gradually started bending. Knowing I caught such a big fish it now seems funny, but I swore that all I had was a log on my line. I really figured it was some more debris floating down the river.

So I started reelin' it in, sort of cussing at it, figuring I was gonna lose some tackle. I got it up to the dock and my eyes almost fell out of my head when I saw it was a fish. I just kind of leaned over the dock and stuck my hand down, grabbed it, and pulled it up on the dock. He started flippin' around and I smacked it on the head. I stomped on him.

The fish had the hook swallowed. We found it in his bladder. My neighbor claims when they're hooked way down like that, and maybe feeling pain, they sort of follow along instead of fighting.

I was fishing with corn. And I was using heavy enough tackle, 40 lb. test monofilament line that my neighbor had given me. I used just a plain hook, a store-bought walleye snelled hook. I was pretty much set up for big fish.

The snow was pretty close to knee-high along the river there. I picked the shortest path home for carrying that fish. I was on foot, fishing only two or three blocks from home. I always walked down there. So I just picked up that catfish, threw him on my shoulder, and started running home. Hauling nearly 40 pounds on my shoulder got pretty tiring, especially since I wasn't all that big then—16 years old. As I was going home there were a lot of cars stopping to look. I had to cross one busy street.

All I wanted to do was to get home and show my parents. My mom was looking out the kitchen window when I came running down the sidewalk with my fish. I guess she asked my dad, "Now what's he coming home with?"

I weighed the fish on our bathroom scale. Then I looked up the Minnesota record for channel cats and found that it was 37 pounds. My fish seemed bigger. So my mom called the *Star*, and they came out and photographed it. They were really nice, and they gave me a lot of space in the paper. Joe Hennessy, outdoor writer for the *Star*, put it together.

The fish had to be officially weighed. That was done at Hamel, Minnesota, at a bait shop that had official scales. 38 pounds!

I had gone down to the river that day to catch something I could mount. I wanted taxidermy practice. So I mounted my record catfish and have it in my basement.

So many people around the Twin Cities think the Mississippi holds nothing but carp. Well, I've spent a lot of time down there, and I know better!

86

F. H. "Mac" McArdle
Pelican Rapids Warden

Mac came to the Pelican Rapids area in December, 1937 as an upstart game warden. During the next 40-plus years he became a respected and well-known outdoorsman.

He had been working on the police force in Hastings. "I felt that being up north as a game warden was a little more in my line," Mac told me. "There was a big shake-up in the warden service in '36 or '37. Many were transferred and some were laid off. New ones were appointed. In this area of Minnesota—Moorhead, Breckenridge, Perham, Fergus Falls, and other towns—16 wardens were involved."

At the age of 84, Frederick Howell McArdle was the only one left of that whole bunch.

Spearers Encounter Warden Bob Streich—
Buried in the Sand!

This happened back in the drought years, the late 1930's, when the lakes were low. There's a creek that runs between Battle Lake and Stuart Lake. And the walleyes would come up there so thick in the spring that you could step on a fish every step across that creek! There were thousands of 'em. And big ones!

It was a hard place for a warden to get up to. Bob Streich was on the scene then. He was a very hard-working warden but not always well liked. He could be a little hot-headed. Anyway, he said, "You guys bury me in the sand, and then get back."

So we scooped out a hole, right by the creek, and buried Bob in the sand. Just his face was stickin' out! Another warden and I got in back of a nearby garage. Then we waited. About two o'clock in

the morning two old guys came out there to get some fish. They just had a little pencil-like flashlight which only showed a little yellow beam. You didn't need much light.

So one guy was in the creek. He had 4-buckle overshoes on. And he was scoopin' the fish out with his hands. He'd flip those walleyes out on shore, and the other guy was sackin' 'em up. Well, this guy on shore was feelin' along the ground for fish, and he put his hand right square on Streich's face! And he hollered for his partner in the creek.

About that time Streich reached out of the sand and grabbed him. And you could hear that guy holler clear across the lake. Imagine a face, and then a hand, comin' out of that sand at two in the morning!

Loudmouth Bay

There's a bay on Lake Crystal where the crappies spawn in the spring. They go in there after the ice is out, when we've had a few warm days.

There were some guys from the Cities who had cottages on the north side of Lake Lida, which connects with Crystal. They'd go over to Crystal and catch crappies in that bay. Then they'd tell everyone how they "murdered" 'em. They always "slaughtered" 'em over there.

So old Gus Strand, who had Strand's Resort on Crystal, told me about it. Then I went up to Detroit Lakes and got an order to close it as a spawning area. Gus helped me post it.

These guys came back to fish and it was posted. They had talked too much! Gus called that place "Loudmouth Bay." And they still call it that today.

Poachers at Little Pine Lake

One time I was workin' with Paul Krueger. He's the warden over at Perham. He's a nice guy. In fact I helped break him in. We worked together quite a lot.

Little Pine Lake, north of Perham, is another place where a lot of pike come up a stream in the spring. So Paul and I were out there watchin' for spearers. We had to be on opposite sides of the river, 'cause you never knew which side the poachers would pick.

Two guys came along. It happened that Paul was on the side where the guy was getting the fish. The other guy was standing on the bridge—watching 'im. I saw that guy standing on the bridge there, so I sneaked up on him. He was busy watchin' his buddy spearing and didn't see me. I got up to him and told him to shut up, so he wouldn't tip his buddy off.

Meanwhile Paul had gotten close to the guy who was getting the fish. He was spearing fish and Paul was right there with the sack! The guy was actually handing fish up to the warden! Paul said to him, "I think you've got enough fish now."

And the guy, who was so interested in those fish, said, "No. Let me get that big son-of-a-bitch first!"

We took 'em in.

Walkie-Talkies and Fred Johnson's Cousin

I can remember when we first got the walkie-talkies. It was spring spearing time, probably somewhere in the late forties. We went over the Pomme de Terre River, where Highway #55 crosses it. Fred Johnson, the warden from Ashby, was along that time.

Every car that came along there would stop. They'd look at the fish. About 75 percent of 'em made no attempt to get any. They just looked.

Well, I laid on the hillside with binoculars and a walkie-talkie. And we had a car some distance up the road, on each side of the Pomme de Terre, so we could stop somebody going either way. From my position up on the hill, I watched a guy stop there and shoot a fish. I watched him hide it in the cattails. It was a good-sized northern.

I tipped off the others and they stopped this guy's car. Then I directed them to where the fish was in the cattails—with the walkie-talkie. So they found the fish.

And here the guy was Fred Johnson's cousin! But that didn't make any difference. They took him in to court at Ashby the next day. He was fined $25. And he said, "Fred, I don't mind the $25, but I'll give you $25 more if you'll tell me how you caught me!"

Netting the Netters

It seems like years ago we found more illegal nets in the lakes than we do now. I know that back then it was much easier to find where netting was going on. You see, there were very few boat trailers around. If you found a boat pulled up on shore someplace,

Before "Mac" was born! An 1884 catch of largemouth bass from Detroit Lake. (Minnesota Historical Society)

or back in a culvert, you knew darn well somebody was holding it there for a reason.

We'd put a little stone or something on the bow of the boat to mark it, so we'd know if it was moved. If we'd come back in a day or two and find the stone gone, we'd know damn well there was a netting job going on somewhere. All we had to do was lay there and wait.

One netting incident involved a prominent resort owner up on Cormorant Lake. I had found out where they were using a boat. I had marked it.

Back then game warden Bob Streich had a small trailer for camping. This one night he dropped me off on the road and I walked down through there along the lake to see if the boat had been moved again. I found that it had been moved. So I reported back to Bob, who had the trailer parked on the south side of the lake, at a spot where we could look across with glasses.

We were gonna go to sleep, but Bob was worried about getting up on time. I told him I had that instinct for wakin' up when I made up my mind to. I said, "Don't worry. I'll get you up."

So I woke up when it was just breakin' daylight. We sat there lookin' out, just in time to see those guys running their net. They were on one side of the lake and we were on the other. And Bob was dancin' up and down. "How are we gonna get them?" He was wild. Maybe he was singin' "If I had the wings of an angel...."

I said, "Oh, hell. Cool down. We'll get 'em. We'll go to Lake Park and call for a search warrant for the place."

We did that. We called Judge Centerwall at Detroit Lakes, but had to wait awhile to get him out of bed. They finally brought the papers down.

The others went in the house and I went back to the shed, which I had passed by the night before. Now it was locked! They came out of the house but didn't find anything. And I said, "Where's the key to this garage?" It had an old cheap padlock on it.

The guy stuttered, "It don't belong to me. I don't have the key." I said, "The hell it don't! It was open last night!"

There was a pile of stovewood there by the shed. And I picked up a piece in my hand. I knew if I hit that cheap padlock a good rap it would flop open. But he started yellin', "I'll get the key. I'll get the key!"

Well, I hit it anyway, before he got the key. I shoved the door open and here were two tubs of pike—still in the gill net. This was quite a while back. But I think even back then they paid $300 apiece!

Royal Karels, Bassmaster

Royal Karels is one of Minnesota's top fishing guides, a skilled all-around angler who specializes in outwitting largemough bass. Trademarks of this Brainerd school teacher-guide are beard, cigar, crazy hat, and a perennial tradition of being among the first with a fish house over Garrison Reef at Mille Lacs shortly after freeze-up.

Royal's countless exploits on the water, his proficiency with language, and a keen sense of humor give rise to all kinds of fishing stories, including the following narratives.

Shooting Down a Shakespeare Mouse

The greatest story teller I ever heard was my grandfather, Earl Currier, who ran a resort on Shirt Lake in the Deerwood-Bay Lake area. He had a million fishing and hunting stories and got to be a famous BSer. Guys would come to his place to rent a boat at 2 in the afternoon and never get fishin'. They'd listen to his stories! He liked to brag about being a good shot with a gun—pistol, rifle, or shotgun—"the greatest shot that ever was."

When I was a boy I'd spend my summers at Currier's Resort. My grandfather's the one who got me interested in bass fishing. I'd go out twice a day, every day, summer after summer.

This one morning, when I was about 11 years old, I was out bass fishing. It was at the south end of Shirt Lake over toward Harry Nelson's, where two bays ran under high-line wires that stretched from farm to farm. For some reason I look up and see a lure hanging from the wires, about 30 feet above the water. Somebody had gotten it tangled in the wires, broke the line off, and gone home. It hadn't been there the day before. Strangely enough, the lure was a Shakespeare mouse with stripes—the Shakespeare Tiger Mouse, my favorite lure!

At noon I went back to the resort and told my grandfather about the mouse hanging from the wires. "Hell," he said, "We'll go over and get it."

I said, "How are we gonna get it?"

He said, "I'll shoot it down."

He told me he'd get his .22 rifle, I should row him over there, and he'd shoot the lure down from the wires. I wondered about that!

So I rowed him over there. There's a slight chop on the water and the boat's rocking. And here's my grandfather with his .22. He says, "Swing 'er around and pull 'er out from under the wires at a slight angle."

Now in those days everybody used that heavy black 25 and 30-pound test nylon line. The line this mouse was hanging from had about a 10-inch wire leader. That's what he shoots at. He snaps the gun up, aims—bang!—and the wire leader kinks. He hit the wire leader and it kinked into a V-shape. He ejected the shell and grumbled, "Gol damn..."

So he fires again—bang!—and down comes the plug! He snapped the wire leader on that second shot. The plug hits the water, he puts his gun down and says, "There's your plug. Pick it up and let's get outta here!"

I never questioned his shooting ability again!

Bass Plugs on Rabbit Lake
Waylaying the Old Man

Bass fishing is a sport where you've got to be super cautious because there's so much casting. It's a lot different from trolling for walleyes. In bass fishing, or any other fishing where hooks are flying around, you can't be too careful. I know what it's like to take people to the hospital for emergency hook removals. A good guide cautions his customers but that sometimes fails. Some people are bound to be reckless. I've got a couple stories to illustrate what I mean, both from Rabbit Lake near Crosby.

This one time I'm moving from one spot to another during a guiding trip. I had a father and son team along, and this teenage boy was really reckless. He'd cast where he wasn't supposed to. He didn't retrieve right. In other words, he was a nuisance, one of those kids who wouldn't listen.

94

Anyway, we're heading across the lake, barrelling along, and he
lets his line out—on purpose! And we were really moving, wide
open with a 35-horse motor. So there was one helluva pull on his
lure. I slowed down and he suddenly yanked as hard as he could.
That plug came whistling through the air—I couldn't see it but I
could hear it—right by my ear and it plunks into his dad's back.
Two barbs of a treble hook were buried in the guy's back, and the
third one was somehow caught in his skin, too. They went through
his shirt and into the flesh. How all three hooks dug in I don't
know. But the hook turned somehow and maybe the guy moved at
just the wrong time.

I cut the line and told them we were only several miles from
Crosby where we'd go to the hospital to get the lure out and to get
the guy a tetanus shot. And the guy shot back at me, "Absolutely
not! I won't hear of it! You can take it out yourself."

I said, "No. I don't perform these operations in the boat. Thank
you. We're going in. You have to get a tetanus shot anyway."

But he starts tellin' me how he was in World War II, he's a very
tough guy, he's been through it all, and this little hook thing in his

back was gonna be no problem. Well, I fought with him as long as I could and finally said the hell with it. I told him I'd take it out. And he said, "Absolutely. You don't know how tough I am!"

I said, "Fine."

And the kid is up there kind of smirking. He's obnoxious as hell and could care less about the whole deal.

The guy said, "Just yank 'er out!"

So I clamped down with my pliers, put my feet on the seat, and as I yanked the guy let out a blood-curdling scream that you could have heard at the Crosby hospital! I have never heard anybody scream that loud in my life. The guy wasn't as tough as he thought he was. He turned really pale and almost passed out. And you know, his back wasn't that bad. It drew a little blood, but not that bad.

He agreed to go in and I reminded him to get a tetanus shot. I don't know if he ever got that shot. And, for all I know, he maybe never came back to Minnesota again. He did say he felt fine when we got back to the resort.

I got those hooks out in a hurry, like the guy wanted, but it's the wrong way. I'll guarantee you that!

Around the same time, a year or two either way, I had another father and son along on a guiding trip. The kid was in his teens and was as contrary as they come. He wouldn't follow directions. He was impatient. And he was careless. He's in the bow of the boat and his dad's in the middle.

The kid swings his rod back, makes a side-arm cast, and hits his dad in the back of the head with a Water-Gator and knocks him out cold! The plug bounced off his head without hooking him, but the guy sagged right to his knees—boom! So he's layin' on the bottom of the boat and doesn't even move for about a second. Then he shakes his head, gets up, holds his head, and seems very groggy. He's seein' stars! "Gee. What happened?" he asked.

I just looked at the kid. Let him explain it, I thought.

Right when the lure hit the guy's head the kid's thumb flew off the spool of his reel and he got the biggest backlash you ever saw, a terrifice bird's nest. So when his dad asked what happened he said, "Look what you made me do to my reel! Look what you made me do!" He made it sound like his dad caused the backlash by sticking his head in the way of the lure.

I think it was the worst backlash I ever saw. And the old man couldn't even see it because he was seein' nothin' but stars. But what compassion that kid had for his father. He damn near killed him with a Water-Gator and then blames him for a backlash!

A Giant Bullfrog and Bass Near the Boat

One time Rodney Romine, another guide, and I went along with Gene King from St. Louis, Missouri, who's quite a frog fisherman in shallow water on North Long. Gene knew the reeds really well. He'd spend weeks up here fishing in the summer time.

I hadn't fished the reeds on North Long that often. Guess it wasn't my style. But we got in there with Gene and were having a good time. We'd have bets on fish, another thing I didn't do much. And the fish were there. I could see bass, and I was astounded that they were that close. I said, "There's bass," and Rodney flips his frog out and catches one, just a few feet from the boat. I always assumed that if a bass could see me like that he wouldn't bite. That's usually the case, but not that day.

This Gene King and Rod were throwing short 10 and 12-foot casts, while I was throwing way out of sight. Those guys were yankin' in bass like crazy and pretty soon we had about 15 bass. So we took off and hit a couple more spots. We were having a good time and had about the limit. It was time to quit.

Now I've got on the biggest frog in the box, just goofin' around trying to catch a big bass. I kidded Rod and Gene about catching the biggest one. This one time I flipped it out and was pulling it in when there was a huge swirl. Something grabbed my frog, I fed it a little line, then set the hook and missed it. I said, "Well, that son-of-a-gun!"

After losing that fish I wound up most of my line, put the rod back over my head, and I beat the water with the frog just as hard as I could. The water flew three feet in the air. And when the frog hit the water, that very second, the fish hit it again! It was just like throwing a 40-pound rock in the water. I yanked, pulled the frog out of the fish's mouth, and the fish got away!

So with my rod still up in the air I came right back down with it again, with all my might, and it was like throwing a washtub full of rocks in there! When that big frog hit the water this fish jumps on it immediately! I yanked again, missed it again, and this time he got my frog and swam away. This all happened in a matter of seconds.

Now whoever heard of hitting the water with that kind of force and getting a fish to bite? I was just goofing around, beating that frog on the water after losing a fish, and everything exploded. I hit that water so hard you couldn't even see. Water was flyin' all over. But each time, instantaneously, this fish was on that big frog. And I didn't have more than three or four feet of line out beyond the tip of my rod! It happened so fast I never saw the fish. It could have been a big bass, a northern, or even a dogfish. But it was big. Hell, it had to be big because that frog was a pounder! It was a giant bullfrog!

Rod and Gene couldn't believe it. It was so contrary to all we hear about laying the bait in there gently to avoid spooking fish.

Peter Miravelle and Royal Karels
Disaster-prone Bassing Duo?

One fellow I'll never forget was Peter Miravelle—not a Scandinavian! He's from St. Louis and has fished with me a lot. His business is packaging—plastic bags, boxes, that type of thing. Now this guy's been in on some wonderful bass fishing trips with me, but he's also been along when bad things happened. Every year, if I encounter disaster on one of my guide trips he's along! I'll tell you what I mean.

A few years ago at North Long Lake we came to shore after our fishing trip. I jumped in the car, backed it up to the landing, and as I'm backing up I know something is wrong. I jump out, look, and here my boat trailer's been stolen! So I have Peter wait with the boat while I go into town to get another trailer. Not much to that story. But it's only the beginning of a series of disasters.

Another year we go to the Mississippi River to fish smallmouth bass. We're on a landing that everybody uses, but it's adjacent to some property whose owners think they control the landing. People from Brainerd have fished there for years. But while we're out fishing these raving people let the air out of two of my tires! So I'm in trouble. I go to jack the car up and the jack doesn't work. In order to get the spare on we had to dig the dirt out from under a tire—by hand! Finally, after an hour and a half or two hours we get one good tire on. So I made it up the hill with three good tires and we limped back to town.

Another time we go to North Long Lake and the water's extremely low. You had to see this to believe it, but the sand was hard and you could back a boat way out over the shallow water, even with a 2-wheel drive. I've driven my Suburban way out in

the lake many times. I take my shoes and socks off, push the boat off the trailer, and drive back to the landing. I've had to back out two blocks in the lake because of shallow water.

That's how we did it the first day. But the second day we went to North Long Miravelle says, "Why get out of the car? Give 'er a turn, back it right up to the dock, I'll hold the boat, and you can drive right out."

That sounds good to me, so I back the boat over to the dock, he hangs onto the boat, but the boat won't come off the trailer. I spin my tires, just a little, and I break through the sand. I mean it dropped in all the way to the axle. So there's my car—the rear end mired down and the front end sticking up. It looked like it was headed for the Moon!

The guy from the resort says, "No problem. I'll get my tractor and pull it out."

He backs in with his tractor, hooks his chain to my car, and goes to give it a pull. My car didn't move, he spun his wheels, and there was his tractor looking like my car, like it was ready to be launched! The resorter then says, "Go fishing. Don't worry about it. I'll get a wrecker and you'll be ready to go when you get back."

Now that was my third Miravelle incident. And that one cost me a lot of money. I had to pay to get the tractor out of the lake, and also to pull my car out. And Miravelle's laughin' like hell. I had to laugh too because so many stupid things had happened when he's along—my stolen trailer, the flat tires, and now getting stuck in the lake.

We're goin' home that evening, heading north on #371 toward Brainerd. There's a camper up ahead of us with its back door swinging open. Suddenly one of these small party type plastic coolers flies out of their camper and gets wedged under my front axle. I couldn't dodge it because there were cars in the left lane. And I wasn't about to go in the ditch.

So I hit that cooler, made of hard plastic, and push it up the highway so hard and so fast that I wear one whole side off it. And it's making one helluva scraping noise as we move down the road! There must have been 50 people at this campground on North Long Lake all looking at us and wondering what the hell is going on. It's making a tremendous amount of noise.

I stop and finally shake this cooler out from under the car, when up pulls this camper. And a woman who weighs at least three hundred pounds and her husband, who was just as big, both jump out and call me every rotten name in the book for running over their cooler—that I couldn't have missed! I'd have had to roll my car or smash into someone else to avoid it.

They called me every lousy name you can think of. And Miravelle is by now in stitches. My car had been stuck, the tractor got stuck, we run over a Coke cooler, and these people are ready to kill me. I'm standing there like a dummy apologizing for ruining their cooler. They finally grabbed it out of my hands, roared down the highway, and I'm standing there with my mouth open.

Every time Peter Miravelle and I begin a fishing trip, one of us asks, "What's it gonna be this time?"

Ron Weber, The Rapala Man

Ron Weber is President of the Minnesota-based Normark Corporation which markets the famous Rapala. This light minnow-like plug is one of the most widely used artificial baits in the entire fishing world. Ron tells some fascinating stories about the Rapala's rise to fame.

"They're Using That Finnish Plug"
Ron Weber Meets the Rapala

My first introduction to the Rapala came on a trip into Canada in summer of 1959. I was with my wife, Mary Ann, and another couple, Donna and Hartley Schilling, friends of ours from Duluth. Duluth's my home town.

In Duluth I stopped to visit George Balmer, a friend of mine who lived right across the road from Pike Lake, which is right on the outskirts of town. It's not much of a resort lake, and it isn't well-known as a fishing lake at all. George asked me, "Why in the world are you goin' all the way into Canada for fishing? Pike Lake is producing walleyes six and eight pounds!"

I told him I couldn't imagine that kind of fishing in Pike Lake. But he said, "Well, they're getting 'em there!"

I asked him, "How are they catching them?"

And George said, "They're using that Finnish plug." That was the first mention I ever heard of the Rapala.

After that we proceeded on up to Dryden, Ontario, to Gull Wing Lake. There's a resort up there, Gull Wing Lodge, which was run by a fellow named Bill Smith and his brother-in-law Al Wallin. It was our first trip up there.

I fished for a day or two and caught a few lake trout. Then Al suggested that he and I go over to an adjoining lake, Lake Bluett, to catch some walleyes. I thought that was a good idea so we went over there, but it turned out to be very, very windy. We spent most of the day sitting on the beach! Finally the wind went down, though, and we got on the lake in late afternoon.

The fishing was pretty slow. We were trying the usual lures, the old standbys. Then Al said, "I've got to bring back walleyes for a camp feed. We need some fish. It's gonna get dark here pretty soon and we'll have to start back. I hate to do this, but this is the last Rapala I have. I'm gonna tie it on and use it. There's big northerns in this lake, though, and one might bite it off."

He explained to me that you couldn't use a wire leader with a Rapala because of its light action. "If a northern hits one," he said, "most of the time you'll lose it."

I asked him if that was the lure from Finland and he said yes, it was. I was very interested because now, in a matter of three or four days, I had heard of this lure twice! And Al was about to show me how it worked.

We started fishing, and I could see a big submerged rock off this point. Every time we went by there Al would get a walleye on that Rapala! We were trolling, with Al running the motor. I tried Spoon-plugs, River Runts, Lazy Ikes, and various lures that usually worked for walleyes back then, and I'd get a fish once in a while. But Al would get one on every pass. I could predict when he'd get a strike. The boat would go by that rock and I knew within three seconds he'd have another walleye.

I couldn't believe all this, so I started asking him about the Rapala. Al told me his uncle was with the American consulate in Helsinki. He was from northern Minnesota and could speak Finnish. When he came back to the States he brought some of these lures with him. The Finns had been using them on their lakes, for brown trout, salmon, and northerns. I guess the uncle had sent Al a dozen lures and this was the last one he had. The northerns kept biting 'em off!

The one Al used was the 11S model, a silver floating Rapala. A few minor changes were made later on, but it was virtually the same lure that Normark would eventually distribute. I asked Al if he knew where I could get some Rapalas. He said no, he didn't.

Well, we loaded up on walleyes on that Bluett Lake trip, but Al caught most of them on his last Rapala. We went back to camp that night and here a fella had come in with a nice big string of lake trout. He was telling me what a good day he had and took me

102

Ron Weber first encountered the Rapala on a Canadian fishing trip in 1959. Soon that "Finnish plug" would be world-famous.

down to show me his fish. I asked him what he caught them on and he said, "sucker meat!"

Later on that night we went to the dining room in the lodge and ran into this guy again. He had a couple martinis under his belt and was a lot more jovial. He came over to me and said, "I feel bad about something. I told you a fish story. Actually we caught those lake trout on that Finlander plug."

So I asked him where he got his lures. He said, "In Duluth, from the fella that owns Dove Clothing, a guy named Alex Kyyhkynen. He was in Finland and brought a bunch of Finnish stuff back with him, including quite a few Rapalas. He'll sell you one or two if you go in the store and ask for them. He's got 'em under the counter there."

Naturally, when I went back to Duluth I stopped to buy a couple Rapalas from this Alex and asked him if he knew where I could get more. He was somewhat suspicious and asked me why I wanted that information. I told him I was in the fishing tackle business, a manufacturer's rep, and that I might be interested in doing some business with Rapalas. And he said something like, "No, you'll just take 'em and pretty soon they'll be in all the discount houses and all over. I don't want anything to do with that. Do you want to buy these two lures or don't you?"

I said, "Yes, I'd like to buy 'em!" This was all in the summer of 1959, early July.

With Ray Ostrom and Upperman Bucktails
Rapalas on Trial at Mille Lacs

I told Ray Ostrom about my first experience with Rapalas in Canada. Ray had Ostrom's Marine and Sporting Goods on 36 East Lake Street in Minneapolis. At that time I was a tackle manufacturer's rep, for Pflueger rods and reels, Gladding line, and Prescott spinners. I was just a one-man rep.

I had bought these two Rapalas in Duluth, showed them to Ray, and told him I wanted to give them a try up north. I'd been doing a little fishing with them myself, around the Cities, and had excellent luck. Ray and I were fishing friends and he said, "Sure, I'll go along." So we went up to Jack's Twin Bay Resort on Mille Lacs, Jack Maciosek's place. Jack was an old friend of Ray's. He was originally from Wisconsin, but he moved to the Cities for a period following World War II. That's when Ray got to know him, because he came into the sport shop. They talked fishing and went fishing together. After he acquired the resort Ray kept in contact with him.

So we went up to Mille Lacs. At that time Ray and I were fishing with jigs a great deal. Our favorite was the Upperman Bucktail. That black Upperman jig was a hot bait on the lake then. We fished it plain then and still fish it without bait today. We each rigged two rods, one with a black Upperman, the other with a

The Original Floating Rapala

Invented by Laurie Rapala of Finland, "discovered" in 1959 by Ron Weber. Ron and Minneapolis tackle seller Ray Ostrom soon started the Normark Corp. which markets the lure.

Rapala. These were silver Rapalas, size 11, with three treble hooks.

Our idea was to head for what we thought would be a good reef or hot spot for jigging. We'd troll around there with the Rapala until we caught fish, then we'd stop and anchor for casting with jigs. We used the Rapala when trolling and scouting for fish. If we wanted to try a new area we'd troll through it with the Rapala, looking for concentrations of walleyes. We'd put a split shot ahead of the Rapala and fished mainly in 10 to 12 feet of water. This was probably the end of July, midsummer of 1959.

We went out around noon and fished until dark, so it was a good half-day's fishing. We didn't break any records but we thought we did well for that time of year in shallow water. There was a limit of walleyes, our six apiece, and we had thrown back maybe six or eight. When we got in I said to Ray, "I just kept track. We actually caught more fish on the Rapalas than we did on the jigs. We fished the Rapala about 25 percent of the time but it caught about 60 percent of our fish!"

The Rapala would later become very famous as an evening and night-fishing bait, but this was daytime fishing! Ray thought about my statistics and said, "You're right. For the amount of time we fished it, the Rapala far out-produced the jigs." And then he added, "You know, I never thought I'd see a lure used on Mille Lacs that would out-produce a black Upperman jig!" He was pretty enthused.

I told Ray I was going to bring some of these lures into the country for a try at marketing them. He said he'd be interested in bringing some into his store. So I contacted Finland's trade council and established a relationship with the Rapala family. I originally bought 500 lures, which I put into several tackle shops in the Minneapolis area. That's how it all started.

A Sturgeon Record, Anybody?

The largest fish in Minnesota waters is the lake sturgeon (Acipenser fulvescens). Sometimes called rock sturgeon, these huge elongate fish have reached weights in excess of 200 pounds in Minnesota. In the late 1800's, sturgeon were so plentiful in Lake of the Woods they were considered a nuisance by commercial fishermen after walleyes with pound nets. Special barges were built for hauling them away!

The range of lake sturgeon in Minnesota was never extensive. Their populations declined rapidly after the turn of the century, most probably because of overfishing and pollution.

While preparing this book I set out to learn about some of the largest sturgeon ever taken from Minnesota waters. My research proved to be most interesting and resulted in the following stories behind five trophy sturgeon. But none of these fish qualifies as a legitimate state angling record. Therefore, at least in this book, the Minnesota angling record for lake sturgeon is up for grabs!

That Old 236-pound Sturgeon "Record"

For as long as I could remember, the Minnesota record for lake sturgeon had stood at 236 pounds and was taken from Lake of the Woods in 1911 by a mysterious "angler unknown." I had never read stories about this catch and began to wonder about its authenticity. How could an unknown hold a fishing record? Was this fish ever caught? If so, was it taken on hook and line?

I found some answers where I expected them to be, in 1911 issues of the weekly *Warroad Plaindealer*, forerunner of the *Warroad Pioneer*. On June 15, 1911 the *Plaindealer* ran the following front-page report entitled "The Biggest Sturgeon":

"The largest sturgeon ever caught in Lake of the Woods—as far as anyone here knows—was brought in on the Isobel the first part of the week. It was caught near Long Point by Louis Palm and his

107

assistant Fred Peterson, who had quite a time getting the big fellow into the boat. He weighed 236 pounds, and dressed 120 pounds, the big difference being because of about fifty pounds of extra fat inside of it. It measured about eight feet.

"Sturgeons approaching 200 pounds have been caught before, and some even longer than this one, but this is the heaviest."

"A large sturgeon like this one is not as valuable as smaller ones, because they contain no caviar."

It seems most improbable that Captain Palm and Fred Peterson were out on a sport fishing trip with hook and line when they caught this big sturgeon. It appears more likely that they were engaged in commercial fishing. You see, the Isobel was a steamer, sometimes used as an excursion boat, with apparent commercial fishing ties to Oak Island fisheries and the Armstrong Trading Co. of Warroad.

Not long after the 236-pounder was brought into Warroad, the *Plaindealer* reported on another "largest sturgeon," larger in dressed weight, a measure important to commercial fishermen. A 213-pounder, this fish was put on display at a commercial fishing business site in Warroad. Here is that story as reported in the *Warroad Plaindealer* on Thursday, July 6, 1911, under the heading "213 lb. Sturgeon":

"The steamer Isobel landed here on Thursday, from Oak Island fisheries, with the largest sturgeon ever known to be caught in Lake of the Woods. It weighed 10 pounds more than the one caught some three weeks ago. This fellow dressed 130 lbs. without head or tail and measured 4 feet in circumference at the fleshiest part and 5 feet long. The immense size of the fish is drawing large crowds at the Armstrong Trading Co. fish house."

In 1911 the Armstrong Trading Co. was advertising "fish to the consumer." If purchased in lots of 100 pounds or more, you could buy whitefish for 7 cents per pound, yellow pike (walleyes) for 7 cents, jackfish (northerns) for 4 cents, goldeyes and buffalo for 1 cent, and sturgeon for 15 cents per pound. For smaller orders you'd add 1/2 cent per pound to the above prices. And there was a 2-cent per pound additional charge on all fish except buffalo and goldeyes if they were to be shipped outside of Roseau and northern Beltrami counties.

Incidentally, caviar was selling for $1.50 per pound.

Again, it is highly doubtful that lake men Palm and Peterson were sport fishing when they boated their 236-pound sturgeon.

"Bottle Bass?" These happy turn-of-the-century sturgeon fishermen are passing the "bait." (Minnesota Historical Society)

Their concern was saleable poundage of dressed fish. Perhaps they "caught" the state's largest sturgeon ever reported. But that hardly qualifies them for a Minnesota angling record.

225-pound Sturgeon Found Dead in Rush Lake

Perhaps the second largest lake sturgeon ever reported in Minnesota, at least after 1900, was a 225-pounder found dying in Rush Lake near Lake City in July, 1947. According to a report by outdoor writer Lytton Taylor in the *St. Paul Dispatch* on July 15, 1947, the fish was discovered by a Steve Sanders, 1173 Arcade St., St. Paul.

Lytton noted that the fish was very likely dying of old age and that fisheries authorities were curious about just how old it was. "Sturgeons do not reach maturity until they are 15 to 22 years old and their reputed life span of 100 years does not seem unreasonable," he speculated.

A photo of Mr. Sanders and the huge 225-pound lake sturgeon accompanied Lytton Taylor's newspaper article.

176-pound Sturgeon From White Earth Lake, Becker County, "Killed in Shallow Water"

Another giant sturgeon found dying was killed by an Indian boy named Frank LeQuier in White Earth Lake, Becker County, just north of Detroit Lakes. The fish was discovered on a shallow bar, stranded, on the morning of May 13, 1926, after Frank and his brother heard splashing noises during the night. Believing it too far gone to live, the boys killed the big sturgeon and dragged it ashore. It was taken to Detroit Lakes, later mounted, and put on display for publicity purposes. The above facts accompanied the display case.

At one time Detroit Lakes promoters billed this big sturgeon as "the largest ever taken in Minnesota waters." It measured 7 feet 3 inches long, 38 inches in circumference, and weighed 176 pounds.

A 162-pound "Rainy River" Sturgeon
Hook 'n Line?

The 236-pound "record" sturgeon and a 213-pounder were almost certainly taken by commercial fishing methods in Lake of the

110

Woods decades ago. The 225-pounder was found dying in Rush Lake. And the 176-pound lunker from near Detroit Lakes was killed in shallow water. Obviously these weren't angling records. So who caught the Minnesota record lake sturgeon?

I thought I found the true record while searching DNR Fisheries files in St. Paul. An Associated Press report indicated that on May 15, 1968 Allen Knaeble of Big Falls, Minnesota took a 162.5-pound lake sturgeon from the Rainy River by "angling." A separate DNR memo, dated June 12, 1968, drew attention to this same big fish, indicating it was weighed at the Farmer's Co-op Creamery at Northome and was processed at the Blackduck meat processing plant. The fish measured 6-1/2 feet long, the memo said, and was caught on a nightcrawler and a 30-16 line, whatever that meant. Perhaps it was 30 lb. line on the reel and a 16 lb. test leader. I didn't know.

But here was apparently an angler-caught fish, in modern times, reported and recorded by reliable sources. What a classic story, I thought, so I called Allen Knaeble in Big Falls for a first-hand account. He seemed a little hesitant at first.

Joe Fellegy: "You caught the fish in the Rainy River, huh?"

Allen Knaeble: "Well, yah....It wasn't really caught on hook and line, but sort of....But it wasn't an official hook 'n line catch. I don't want to incriminate....Well, it's been long enough, ten years back. It was kind of a funny deal, I guess."

I had called for a fish story all right. And I got one! Here's the real story about that 162.5-pound sturgeon, as Allen Knaeble tells it.

Actually, the fish was taken from Dead Man Rapids on the Little Fork River. That's upriver from the Rainy, probably about 30 miles, maybe even 40 miles. Both the Big Fork and the Little Fork flow into the Rainy. You can't fish sturgeon legally here in these smaller rivers, but the same fish are legal in the Rainy River.

It was kind of an annual thing. The people had been catching sturgeon there for years, in both the Little Fork and the Big Fork Rivers. Nobody thought much about it. They'd smoke 'em and bring 'em up town. The fish run every spring, but they're hard to see because the river's usually too high. But they're here. I live in Big Falls, and in spring you can see 'em right here in town, in the rapids on the Big Fork River. The old timers had been taking sturgeon out of these rivers for as long as I can remember. I've even heard of them shooting 'em with shotguns!

111

One of the largest fish ever reported in Minnesota, a 176-pound lake or rock sturgeon, from White Earth Lake in Becker County. The fish became stranded in shallow water and killed by young Frank LeQuier (right) on May 13, 1926. (Minnesota Historical Society)

In the spring of 1968 the Little Fork River was low. This one morning, in the middle of May, some guys brought a sturgeon into Big Falls that weighed 90 pounds. They took it from an area of white water on the Little Fork. So a bunch of fellows from town— seven of us—went up there. Sturgeon were all around there. We must have seen 50 or 60! Normally, when the water is high, you just see a tail come out of the water once in a while. But now you could see their big grey bodies all over the place!

It was a small area of the river. They'd drift from a pool into a rapids. They'd start up the rapids. I saw fish there that I know weighed over 200 pounds.

We sat there, on the shore, and watched several of the fish surface. We didn't know what to do. But we had a gaff. So I got in the water with the gaff. I must have been standing there for a half an hour. I missed a number of fish because I couldn't set the gaff into 'em. So we devised a better rig.

We fixed up a handle for the gaff, a piece of hardwood tree about 8 or 10 feet long. We lashed that onto the gaff and tied a rope to it. I had a hold of that wooden handle, standing there in the water. There were three guys out in the water, wading around. The others were on shore, holding onto the rope.

It was hard to see the fish. The water was all white, really turbulent. All of a sudden they'd be there, maybe six of 'em right in front of you. They'd come sliding out of that deep hole and suddenly show up as big grey bodies. I missed a number of fish.

Finally, this big one came up right alongside of me. It actually rubbed against my leg. I just laid that gaff right over his back. I had to shorten my grip on the handle because he was so close. I set the gaff into the fish, right in the area of the dorsal fin. At the same time I hollered, "Pull!"

And the guys on shore pulled! They sunk that gaff in good. She was solid! You see, that was just kind of a home-made gaff, with no barb on it. If they'd a given 'er any slack at all, it would have gotten away. But they pulled, and that big sturgeon just went water skiin' out of the river and up onto the shore!

Now that river was fast. And there were rocks on the bottom. So you had to walk very carefully. When they took off with that fish I didn't want to let go. So I went right along with it! Talk about getting wet! I had gaffed the fish about 50 feet from shore.

So, you see, the only reason I got all the acclaim was that I set the hook into the fish. But there were a bunch of guys in on the catch.

We took the fish down to Huff's Meat Market at Blackduck to have it processed. That's where the game wardens confiscated it at first, because there was no license number on it—something I didn't know we had to have. So we got a license number to put on it.

Anyway, they smoked it there. But the fish was so thick that the initial smoking wasn't enough. It didn't get done. So I brought it home. Then a friend of mine, Curly Wynkoop, a state forester at the time and a good fish smoker, cut it in strips and finished the smoking. Then it was very good. We had a great big feed here in town. It was rich, but delicious.

It wasn't long before everything kind of caught fire. About two weeks later the wardens came around to see where the hell we got that fish. So we had to say it was caught in Rainy River on hook 'n line, 'cause that was the only legal place to have one! I think they realized our story was off base, but they didn't push it too hard. And we never said too much about it, for obvious reasons. The true story never came out, except locally. People around here knew about it, and I think some people in the DNR knew how it was caught, too.

My "fishing" story made the papers, like Blackduck, International Falls, Little Fork, and Northome. I actually took the fish down to the Northome *Record* office, because Northome was my home town. I had just moved away from there at the time.

My wife was just about ready to kill me. People kept calling our place. Ron Schara, from the *Minneapolis Tribune*, called me about a week later. After that it went out over AP and hit the national press! I had relatives of mine see the story in Florida, California, and all over the place.

Ron reported that the catch was made in the Rainy River. He had to. I gave him that story. My big fish bit on a nightcrawler in the Rainy River! One of the Duluth TV stations showed a picture of the fish and reported that it was caught on 3 lb. test line while fishing in a canoe. Now that was really a joke!

It was caught on hook 'n' line, though. Sort of.

A real Minnesota sturgeon record, anybody?

Dick Pence, Whipholt Guide

For years Dick Pence guided out of Huddle's Resort at Whipholt, Minnesota, on the south shore of Leech Lake.

Smelt? Or Shmelt?

You meet all kinds of characters when you're fishin'! If you've guided at all you know that. I had one fellow by the name of Rudy. The last name was German, something like Whittis. He'd take along a fifth of Canadian Club and he'd drink that every day! Every time we went out he'd bring one along.

We had had pretty good fishin' but then it got bad. There was a good walleye hatch a couple years before, so we were gettin' a lot of them about nine inches long. Anyway, this Rudy is about three-fourths gone into the breeze, if you know what I mean. He'd bring in those little walleyes, hoist 'em up, and beller, "Ha! Smelt!" Only he said "Shmelt!" Then he'd throw 'em back.

Well, from then on all those little walleyes were called shmelts. They called 'em shmelt all over Leech Lake!

A Flight To Grand Rapids for Billy Fins

I used to fish a lot with a fellow from southern Illinois. He was a car body engineer, a fellow by the name of Paul Wire. They'd come up here for about three days at a time, and they'd generally fly up. Most of the time they'd land at the Longville airport.

Anyway, they flew up—he and his wife—to go muskie fishing on Leech Lake. This was probably about the twentieth of July, 1953. That was back when I first started fishing with Billy Fins, and it was hard to get baits.

I had told this guy, "You come up and I'll guarantee you your limit of muskies." So they came up and we started fishing. And the darn things wouldn't hit!

I told them, "We need those Billy Fins." Paul said, "What's a Billy Fin?" I said, "A black bucktail." He said, "Where can we get 'em?" And I told him I didn't know!

So he said, "Okay. We'll go get the plane and we'll fly out to where we can get Billy Fins." We were gonna go to the Fuller wholesale store at Park Rapids, where they have a bigger volume of tackle than we have around here. But instead we wound up in

Grand Rapids. We landed at the airport and took one of their cars downtown to the Fuller retail store there.

Let me tell you, they had Billy Fins! They had 'em hanging up on racks. That ceiling seemed like it was 20 feet high. They were up on wires—wa-a-a-a-ay up in the air! So I asked the guy, "What are those baits up there?" The guy says, "Gosh, I don't know. You want me to get 'em down?" I told him, "Get 'em all down." Because I knew what they were!

I asked him how much they cost and I think he said 85 cents. Now they'll run you six or seven dollars for that same bait! There were eight of 'em there and I said we'd take all eight.

Then we flew to Longville and drove back to Huddle's Resort. We took the boat and went back out to the weed bed. We caught three muskies and lost about five more with those Billy Fins in the short time we were out that afternoon. And we came in before sundown, in time for them to go out and eat supper. We each caught our muskie.

And I had to laugh at his wife, Betty. She hooked three different muskies and they'd get off right up by the boat. She didn't have 'em stuck good, see? She didn't yank hard enough. They'd get off and, man, she'd peel off a roll of cuss words a half a mile long! So I told her, "The next time you get one on, let me know right away and I'll help you set that hook." And she said, "Get to settin'!" Well, I gunned the throttle of the engine and tightened up on her line. We got that fish in the boat!

That time we were casting, settin' still on calm water and casting on the edge of the weeds. At one stretch back then I caught 14 muskies on one weed bed in a spot not more than 150 feet long. And I wasn't the only one who caught 'em there! But the water's higher now and those weeds are gone.

Tyin' Knots

I've had it happen many times. I'd teach 'em a knot while going across the lake. This one time a guy was settin' there practicing tyin' knots. I watched and just knew he was gonna throw his knife in the lake. He was tying the knots, cutting 'em off the line, and then throwing 'em over the side of the boat. Pretty soon he laid a knot down and throwed the knife in the lake! Guess he got his throwing mixed up.

Cliff Riggles, Cass Lake Guide

Cliff Riggles is a longtime Cass Lake guide, well known for his ability to find walleyes. Cliff also has many impressive muskie catches to his credit. During the much celebrated muskie rampage at Leech Lake in 1955, Cliff found plenty of muskie action in the Cass Lake area. The following stories involve Cass Lake walleyes and muskies.

A Favorite Guiding Trip on Cass Lake

One of my favorite guiding trips on Cass Lake took place a few years ago, when two elderly retired couples from St. Joe, Missouri drove into Birch Villa Resort to go fishing. They had never been on a Minnesota fishing vacation before. And I'll never forget the questions, the goings on before the trip, and the fishing itself.

These people were really eager to go, but they were afraid that someone was going to take their money. You know the type. Well, it must have taken an hour for me to line things up and to give them a good pitch about going out. They were skeptical and I sort of needed to challenge 'em. I made up my mind that I was going to take them fishing, so I gave them a pretty strong pitch, since our luck had been good on Cass around that time.

On that day my depth finder was haywire, but I didn't really need it. And I had passed up my morning trip because of rain. So I was eager to go and show these people some fishing, but they'd ask about the price of this and that, and then they'd huddle and talk. Then they worried about renting a cabin and not catching fish. As I say, the fishing had been good. But it seemed like they wanted it driven into them somehow that we really stood a good chance of getting walleyes. It was a new place for them and they had never done this kind of fishing before, so they were worried.

Finally they huddled again and decided to go. I told 'em I'd help get their tackle ready. So they opened their trunk. I tell you, they had groceries enough to stay for a month! They had potatoes, and chicken, and hamburger, and onions. You name it and they had it.

Anyway, their tackle was a mess. The reels were dirty from fishin' for mudcats and bullheads. And they needed new line. When they heard that they must have figured I was tossing another gimmick at them. We were still using 20-pound test black line, good line, and I think it sold for about $1.20 a spool. They mulled that over and thought it was pretty high. Five bucks a head for fishing plus another five for line brought my price up to $25 for the two couples. On top of that came the hooks, leaders, and sinkers! And we were using pretty heavy sinkers, fishin' in 35 and 40 feet of water. Well that got 'em shook. But I oiled up their reels, rigged 'em up, and we finally got going about three in the afternoon. It was a nice fall afternoon.

We had quite a ways to go. On the way those folks looked at the scenery and talked about how beautiful the lake was. We went by islands, Cedar Island and Star Island, and it was plain to me that they were enjoying the boat ride. They had never done anything like this before and I could tell they were getting more interested all the time. And that made me feel good, too. So I took my time going across the lake.

We got out to the fishing grounds, and, like I said, my depth finder had quit so I didn't have it along. But I had a marker which I intended to use. We got to the spot and the wind was just right for takin' me down the bar. We got all baited up, got the lines in, and started drifting along.

Pretty soon the one lady in the middle seat got one on. I saw her pole bend and I told her, "You got one hangin' on there." She didn't know it at first but finally she started to crank. It was fighting. It was a good one. So I thought I better wind up my line and get it out of the way. Then I threw out the marker can. And right away one of the guys asked, "Do you think the fish will follow that?" I said, "No. They can't because the can is anchored and standing still. We're drifting away from it!" This shows you how much they knew about walleye fishing. For me it was getting funnier all the time.

Anyway, she was working away with that fish. I just watched for awhile, and then I could see she needed help. The guy in the front of the boat was her husband, and he had to step over another seat to get back to help her. He grabbed a hold of her pole about half way up, with the other hand near the reel. Meanwhile she just struggled away at turning the reel handle. She had a good fish!

Pretty soon the other lady starts reelin' away. She said, "I've got something, too." I told her to take her time. At first I thought they were tangled together with the same fish, but they weren't. They each had fish on. Now, while the husbands were helping their wives, their poles were set down against the side of the boat—with the lines running out! I could see that the situation was a little out of control, but I didn't say anything. I didn't want to upset things while they were hauling in what seemed like big walleyes.

Finally I saw a fish, the first lady's fish. I still couldn't get it with the landing net when I saw that we really had a mess. All four lines—sinkers, hooks, and line—were a real mess!

Then the other fish came around and I finally got both of them in the net at the same time. A 7-pounder and a 4-pounder. Nice walleyes. But there were fish, sinkers, line, everything all tangled together! I threw the whole mess into the boat. And those old people couldn't say enough. They never dreamed they'd start their fishing like this. I wished I had a camera to catch their faces.

Meanwhile, the men's lines were still dragging out there, tangled in the boat with the fish, but still out there. I told 'em to sit down while I untangled the fish. I wanted to get all straightened out before fishing again. And I told them that this was the end of the tangling! "When we catch fish again everybody's gonna have to hang onto his own line and keep it straight," I told 'em.

It must have taken me a quarter hour or more to get things back to normal. By that time we had drifted maybe a quarter of a mile from where we caught the fish. I had just let the boat go, you know. I told 'em we'd have to run back. Well, they couldn't understand that we had moved. They thought the marker was moving!

So we went back and fished. We wound up with a limit of walleyes. They surely weren't all as big as those first ones, but they had nice fish. We went back to shore and they started cleaning fish. I don't think they had handled walleyes before. They started to skin the walleyes, like cleaning bullheads. They'd cut around the gills, then take a pliers and start pulling back. Anyway, they fried fish. And, boy, they were ready to go again the next day. But then we had another rain and storm. She really rained and blew. So those two couples went back to Missouri. But they were gonna come back.

I'll never forget that trip. The things that happened, their discussion of price, and all the things they said! I just enjoyed sitting

120

there and watching 'em. There was no end to their happiness at
the end of that trip.

Big Muskie Catches Angler With Pants Down

Steve Stetz came up here from Oakley, Kansas. He was a good
muskie fisherman, who had just gotten here and was eager to go.
This was gonna be his first trip out after landing here on vacation.

It was the end of July, somewhere in the 1960's. We got up really
early that first morning, a nice-looking day. It was hot and still. No

121

wind at all. So we beat that water to a pulp. We ran all over the lake, but we never saw a muskie, never had a strike. Finally it was getting to be about 9:30 in the morning. We had been out since 5 o'clock.

It was getting hot and we talked about going in for bacon and eggs. We decided to quit—after "one more cast." I made my last cast with no hit, so I wound up and took a drink of water. While Steve was retrieving he had some trouble with his pants. They were loose, shirt tails hangin' out while he was winding in. He wound his jointed Pikie Minnow to the boat and set the rod between his knees so he could loosen his belt and tuck in his shirt. The Pikie Minnow was just barely floating on the water next to the boat.

While Steve was stuffin' in his shirt, and talking about the nice day and everything, whoom! A fish threw water and grabbed that plug! Well, he grabbed the rod with his left hand and was holding his pants with his right hand. Now, he grabbed the rod ahead of the reel, a Pflueger Supreme reel. So when the fish took off, the line unwound through his hand and backlashed the reel. Steve was a pretty religious guy, but he did a little swearin'.

So he dropped his pants and stood there in his shorts. That was the smart thing to do because he was able to get a hold of the reel and sort of recover. The fish was still on, and, luckily, the line went off the reel without snarling tight. Of course, you can imagine that as it unwound the reel handle was turning every which way.

We landed that muskie, and it weighed 37 pounds! I guess that's what you'd call getting caught with your pants down!

Cliff's Biggest Muskie

The biggest muskie I ever caught came from Pike Bay of Cass Lake. It's kind of an odd story. It happened in September, back in the early 1950's when people were less excited about records and weighing big fish.

I took a fellow from Dakota with me. He came through here with a load of fence posts. He had been driving truck most of the night and had to unload right away the next morning. So he was tired, but eager to go fishing.

We were trolling for northerns with Dardevles, along the weeds. The wind came up, blowing from the south. We were kind of on the northwest side and it was getting kind of windy along there.

He was in the front of the boat and I was in the back running the motor.

We had caught a couple small northerns, maybe four-pounders, and had a couple more blocks to go when I said, "We'll go up to the end of this point and we'll head 'er on in." It was getting pretty rough. He was tired and was ready to go in, too.

So I just went a few feet—going pretty fast to keep the boat straight—and man! Something hit hard and I gave 'er a yank. It came out of the water and of course this guy could see it. He said, "My God, you've got a big one now! We'll never get him!"

Well, I told him if the wind didn't blow us into the bulrushes we'd probably be all right. But the wind was blowing us that way and we weren't too far from 'em. Anyway, I got the boat swung the way I wanted it and started the fight. My partner was going to come to the back of the boat to help. But that would have been a mess, with both of us back there, the front of the boat out of the water, and the waves and all. So I told him to stay up there and to get his line in.

Luckily, the fish took off out into the lake, away from the rushes. I was crankin' and trying to handle the boat at the same time. Finally I got out quite a ways and was feeling better because I now had a chance—away from those rushes. Eventually my fish came to the top and boy, he looked big! He was a huge fish. We wrestled him for another ten minutes and finally we got close enough to him and got the gaff hook where it belonged. So I got him into the boat. He thrashed from one end of the boat to the other. But we had him.

We guessed him at 60 pounds. I personally had never been in contact with, or seen a fish like that. I was excited and so was he. I got him on a stringer, after he bled all over the place. I had gaffed him pretty good under the gills. He was just about dead when I put him over the side of the boat.

We decided to fish the rest of the way back in hopes of another big fish. So we started trolling again and pretty soon he hit one. And he really had a tough time of it! This time I was free to handle the boat while he cranked away, gaining and losing ground. A number of times I ran up toward the fish. This fish ran away from the rushes, like mine. I'd run up on him and away he'd go. This went on for about 15 minutes before we got a look at his fish.

By this time the guy was getting all in and nervous, even shaky. But he sure got calmed down and was disappointed when he saw

123

his fish. It wasn't a big muskie at all. Instead it was about an 18-pound northern, which he snagged in the stomach! We got him, too.

Now that was a fishing trip when the last couple blocks on the way to the dock were interesting. We weighed my fish at home. This guy took it with him and had it mounted. The weight, by the way, was 52 pounds. His name was Mueller—I think that's how you spell it—Bud Mueller from South Dakota. He had a lumber yard.

Clarence Luther, Guide for 60 Years

When Clarence Luther began his guiding career, daily limits for walleyes and bass were at least 15, and there was no limit whatsoever on northern pike! A pair of oars and a flat-bottomed wooden boat were standard equipment. For years this Brainerd native boasted of having 39 lakes in his guiding repertoire. Headquartering near Cullen Lake northeast of Nisswa, Clarence Luther was still active after 60 years in business.

"I've Never Fallen In"

There was a guy who used to hunt and fish with me in September and early October. That was back in the early 1920's when the hunting season opened in the middle of September. This fellow, Charlie Everingham, was from Robinson, Illinois. I'd always get him a cabin close by here.

On one October day we went over to Pelican Lake. We had been hunting in the morning, so we had our hunting clothes on, hip boots and all the heavy gear. Anyway, we got out there for fishing and he stands up in this old flat-bottom boat to cast. I said, "Charlie, sit down before you fall out of the boat." And he said, "You've never seen me fall out of a boat yet, have ya?"

Well, as he said that his feet slid, he grabbed me around the neck, and I just laid over flat. I could see his boots go over the side in the neatest dive you ever saw into 15 feet of ice water! I thought that man would never come up. When he did pop up he was at least 20 feet from the boat. I had nothing but oars at that time, but I got the boat over to him. As I got within an arm's length of him his hair was flattening out on the water as he was ready to go down the second time.

I grabbed him by the hair and I lifted him up so I could get hold of his collar. But I couldn't get him into the boat. At that time

Clarence Luther, a guide for more than 60 seasons!

I weighed 149 pounds and this guy stripped at probably 185. And he had all these heavy clothes on! It was clumsy rowing, but I dragged him two blocks to shore. I'm telling you! That was a close call, but I laugh about it now.

That guy came back here every year for the next twenty years and never did I have to tell him what a boat seat was for. He learned that in one hard lesson.

Fred Potthoff's Big Walleyes

For many years Fred Potthoff operated Minnewawa Lodge on Clark Lake. As the years went by he got so he fished nothing but bass. But I can remember taking him on his first walleye trip on Pelican Lake. It was in October and snowing out, back in '36.

We weren't on the lake 15 minutes and he had an 11-pound walleye flopping in the boat! I told Fred that in all my years of guiding I never caught one that big. He said, "Oh, I can do better than this one!" I said, "Fred, it just doesn't happen that way."

So help me, I baited his hook and he came right back with a 12-pounder! He had two walleyes laying there that weighed 23 pounds. And to this day, after 60 years of guiding, I still haven't caught one over 10 pounds.

Gangsters and Machine Guns

Tom McMeekin was a Brainerd boy who eventually became one of the top criminal lawyers in the Midwest. He never cared about fishing too much, but for some years I guided his wife pret' near every weekend.

One weekend he came up from St. Paul and asked me, "Clarence, how would you like to fish with Baby Face Nelson?" I told him I didn't think I'd care to. "You wouldn't? Well, you fished with Mr. So-and-so on Lake Margaret for five days last week. Right?" I said yes. Then he told me. I had fished with Baby Face for five days and didn't know it! Tom said the heat was on and he had to send him somewhere. That was back in the thirties, just before the time they knocked off the First National Bank in Brainerd. Maybe they were casing it when he was here!

Then one time, back in prohibition days, there were nine fellows up here from Illinois. My brother and I took them fishing. They drove a big La Salle sedan, quite a car at that time. When they were getting ready to leave, the one guy said, "Clarence, I'll bet

Clarence Luther began guiding before outboards were popular. Here row-boats are readied for a "tow" on Mille Lacs, 1925. (Minnesota Historical Society)

you don't have any fishermen with cars like this one." I told him I'd seen those cars before. He said, "No, they had different motors. Come here and I'll show you."

So he lifted up the hood and there was a machine gun mounted over the engine! I said, "What the hell?" And he told me, "I'll be honest with you. These are bootleggers from Chicago, on their way to Canada for a load."

We fished with them for a week!

A Day With Doctor Dewey

I remember an interesting day I spent with Dr. Donald Dewey of Owatonna, Minnesota. This was around 1958. It was 18 above that morning in October, colder than the dickens. We wanted to fish walleyes on Gull Lake, specifically a point about four miles across from our landing. It was really foggy, all souped in.

So I told Doc to get in the front of the boat with the compass to guide me while I did the steering. Well, we came out all right, within two hundred yards of where I wanted to be. We had hardly stopped when Doc pulled in a nine-pound walleye. Then I got an

128

eight-pounder, and he got a four-pounder—all within about 20 minutes. Then he said, "Let's go home. I can't take any more of it." So we went back to his cottage and warmed up a little.

Pretty soon Doc suggested we go bass fishing over on Upper Cullen Lake. I thought that was a good idea. So we get up there and he gets a big bass on in the weeds. He was winding away and winding away and all at once he says, "There's something wrong with this reel, Clarence. I can't wind in any more."

I looked at the reel and discovered the problem. He had gloves on, and one finger of a glove got wound up under the level wind of his reel. It was stuck! You can imagine the struggle that followed. Luckily, after chasing the bass all over the weeds, we finally got him—a five pounder.

Gary Korsgaden, "Crappie King"

In the early 1970's Gary Korsgaden dreamed of becoming a career fisherman. Headquartering in the Fargo-Moorhead area, he hounded western Minnesota lakes, entering local fishing tournaments whenever he could. His reputation as a skilled angler spread fast. By the end of the decade Gary had established himself as a real pro fisherman, and was firmly entrenched in outdoor media work.

Murky Water, Gapen's Cockroach, And Giant Crappies

My fishing partner was Roger Zueger from Fargo, North Dakota. It was on a Sunday, August 5, 1979. We went down to our favorite little lake, Prairie Lake, north of Pelican Rapids. It was very warm and muggy, with just the lightest breeze, if any at all. And it was cloudy.

We struck out across the water like we normally do when we crappie fish—bucket full of small crappie minnows; three or four ultra-light rods apiece loaded with 4-pound test line; and tackle boxes full of small jigs, 1/16-ounce and 1/32-ounce jigs. We found a little sunken island with submerged cabbage weeds on top. Roger and I were lookin' at the depth finder and we saw this huge school of crappies all along the weedline. They were down about 8 feet in 22 feet of water.

So we work that area real slowly with the electric trolling motor. I'm standing in the front of the boat, Roger's in the back. I'm casting a 1/16-ounce Bass Buster maribou jig, yellow and white. We're workin' along the edge of the weeds real quietly and carefully, just right, making lots of casts. And not a bite! Not a crappie! This was in the morning. We had gotten there about 8 o'clock. So we take off, go to another spot, and it's the same thing. Nothin'! This was also a good spot, out in the middle of the lake.

After taking a licking there we went back to that first spot. I had looked down in the water and noticed how off-colored it was, sort of green with algae. In that murky water you'd lose that yellow and white maribou jig in no time. So I tied on a bright pink Gapen Cockroach jig, with just the jig head, no body. Then I took the bright yellow body off another Cockroach and put it on with that pink head. You can imagine the contrast—a flashy pink head and this bright yellow body. It really showed up in the water. And with its rubber body it sank a lot slower than the maribou. Roger thought it looked pretty good so he rigged up the same thing. We both had on these odd-colored Cockroach jigs.

He makes a couple casts and hooks into the first crappie of the day. We later found out it weighed three pounds even! So we keep working along there and keep catching crappies, a mess of big fish! We'd get one about every three casts, in this same area that produced nothing earlier. But, you see, these jigs apparently were the right color, they settled more slowly, and that's what the crappies wanted at that time.

We got a lot of fish there, and then we moved into that second spot where we drew a blank earlier. Sure enough. More big crappies, left and right, all along the weed edge. All big ones! These were sunken cabbage weeds, and the fish were right along the edge. Roger and I were betting on the fish, 25 cents a fish. It was his turn to run the motor, so he'd try to pull me away from that weed edge and get himself positioned better, just to needle me.

So I told him, "I'll fix you," and I made a super long cast. The jig didn't sink five feet and it suddenly stopped. I set the hook and thought, "Oh, my God! This is a good one!"

I brought him up and started to see that bright shiny side flash in the murky water. I said, "Roger, get that net under him." I was a little nervous, because Roger had kidded me about not netting my fish. But then he saw it was a big crappie and netted it. What a fish! It turned out to be 3 pounds 5 ounces, my biggest crappie ever!

We had caught this mess of huge crappies, all we wanted, so we headed back. But we decided to stop near shore, still on the lake, to take some pictures. We're getting the camera ready and holding up the two biggest crappies when this boat comes by. This guy went around our boat, just kept looking, and was astounded at the size of those fish.

So we went in to the Crystal Lake Store and weighed the fish. The proprietor couldn't believe it. We had 13 crappies ranging from 2 pounds 9 ounces to 3 pounds 5 ounces.

The following Tuesday I was working in Fargo and thought I'd call the *Forum's* sports writer, Jerry Rafftery, a friend of mine. I was gonna give him a little grief, sort of razz him about the size of those crappies. He answered, and I said something like, "How's it going, Jerry?"

He said, "Good. Where did you get those 3-pound crappies?"

I said, "What do you mean?"

He said, "Well, I talked to one of the guys who works here, and he was out on Prairie Lake and saw your fish."

So Jerry already knew about our crappies. And others soon found out, too. But that didn't make much difference. A week later I had Dave Czanda of the *In Fisherman* staff along, and we couldn't come up with a crappie! Roger and I had made our catch when the conditions were perfect, something we may never see again.

Once we started using those Cockroach jigs we caught fish consistently, all day. It must have been the right combination of everything, weather and bait. We'd cast 'em out and let those jigs settle very slowly with loose line. The trick was to let 'em sink very slowly. When the line stopped sinking we'd set the hook. Those crappies were suspended, five to eight feet down at the edge of the weeds, in about 21 or 22 feet of water. The weedline in that lake goes down to about 17 feet, and the fish were a few feet out from the edge. So our jigs weren't getting near the bottom.

And we didn't get a whole bunch of small crappies in between. We had a couple around 2 pounds and some down to a pound and a half. All good ones!

Playing Hooky

An Unexpected Meeting with the Principal At Little Toad Lake

When I was a senior at Fargo South High I played hooky a lot in order to go fishin', mainly in Minnesota. In the spring of the year I'd be in school for maybe three days a week, and then take the other two off to go fishin'. Any time the weather'd get nice I'd go chase crappies or walleyes.

On this particular day in spring, right after the walleye opener,

my friend Al Olson and I drove over to my folks' lake home on
Little Toad Lake, about 15 miles northeast of Detroit Lakes, Minnesota. Little Toad is a rather unpopular lake—not many people
fish it—but it's a quiet sort of offbeat place to go.

It got really nice and warm out and we decided to skip school
after the first period. I told Al, "Boy, the walleye opener was just
last weekend, and the crappies are up in the shallows spawning.
Little Toad's got some huge crappies in it!"

So I took the cabin key from the coffee cup where my Mom kept
it. We loaded our fishing gear and took off for the lake, in Al's car.

Gapen's Cockroach

Gapen's Cockroach, a popular jig for crappies made by
Gapen's of Big Lake, Minnesota.

The trip went fine, we got the boat and motor all set to go, and
went out. I had about three or four favorite sunken islands that I
liked for walleyes and crappies, and that's where we headed. We
got out there about 11 o'clock.

It was a perfect day of fishing. We caught maybe 15 or 16 nice
big crappies and six or eight walleyes up to 5-1/2 pounds. We
fished until 5:30 or 6 o'clock, about the time you think of heading
home. We had plenty of fish anyway.

There's a small island in the lake. We had been watching a boat
on the other side of that island for the longest time. There were
three guys in the boat, anchored, facing the island, and fishing
away. We got curious so we thought we'd check on them on the
way back, to see how they were doin'.

We motor over there, pull up close to them, and they're still
fishin'. They hadn't turned around yet. We get closer and finally
one of them turns around. I thought Al and I were both going to
faint! We looked at each other and couldn't believe it. The first guy
that turned our way, sitting in the middle of the boat, was Fargo
South's principal, Ed Raymond! Two seconds later the guy in the
front of the boat turns around. He's Charles Cochran, our geography teacher! He looked at us kind of funny-like because Al and I
both skipped his class.

To make matters worse, the guy in the back of the boat turned
out to be our chemistry teacher, Jim Marschke. We had left his
first-hour class after getting an excuse-pass for feeling "sick."

What could we do? We visited with them a little bit, but they didn't mention a word about our being gone from classes. They were drinkin' a few beers and they didn't have a fish! So we gave them the walleyes, but no way would we give them those big crappies. Then Al and I took off, docked the boat, and drove back to Fargo.

We were sweatin' it that night, not knowing what to expect. The next day in geography class Mr. Cochran remarked, "I s'pose those walleyes you gave us should help you out at the end of the quarter." The rest of the class didn't know what he was talking about.

In our first-hour chemistry class Mr. Marschke brought up the same subject. He had a funny look on his face when he said to me, "I guess I can let your 'excused absence' stand, but if you hadn't given us your walleyes you'd be in trouble!"

They knew we were sweatin' things but they let us down pretty easy-like. It sure was a funny deal. Here we were on a lake, miles from anywhere, skipping school and figuring we had it made. Then we run into two of our teachers plus the high school principal! There must be 150 lakes in the Detroit Lakes area, a ton of lakes anyway, and they had to pick Little Toad!

Stan Nelson, From Litchfield

Stan Nelson, one of southern Minnesota's top anglers, guides in the Hutchinson-Dassel-Litchfield-Spicer latitude. Fishing in this region's many lakes often lacks the attention given to action "up north," but Nelson's catches are proof of the fine angling available here. Stan has been a columnist for Ed Gerchy's *Outdoor Outlines* and host of a local television outdoor show.

Little Green Frogs and Big Bass At Ripley Lake

On September 5, 1968 I caught the biggest largemouth bass of the season in Minnesota. I did a lot of frog fishing at that time, especially in fall. I'd pick the little green frogs, the small ones, about an inch and a half long across the back. It's a simple rig, just a number 1/0 hook with a fairly good-sized split shot about a foot above the frog. I'll throw one out and let him settle down alongside the weeds, deep patches of bulrushes. We fish pretty deep water down here, so you might have six or seven feet of water around these bulrushes.

My father-in-law, Ray Bannister, was the one who got me going on that frog fishing. He lived in Litchfield all his life, and he's the one who told me there were some big bass in Lake Ripley. The lake is also noted for its big crappies and bluegills. Northerns, too. I moved to Litchfield in the late 1960's and fished that lake quite a bit. I had never caught anything really exceptional, but I had some 4 to 4-1/2-pound bass.

I went out there this September morning, real early. There was frost on the boat seats. I didn't have a boat of my own at the time, so I rented one at Nistler's Boat Rental, right on the north shore of Lake Ripley. I just rowed out, to a big patch of bulrushes where I had been doing fairly well. The lake has a lot of bulrushes in it.

I had caught a bunch of little frogs. I'd hook 'em through the lips. Well, I started fishin' and pretty soon I caught a bass about five pounds. I thought it was really some fish. But it wasn't long and I landed a six-pounder! I kept fishing and caught fish, bass after bass. They were just wild that morning, and I was getting low on frogs. I had been out since maybe 5:30 or 6 o'clock. About 8:15 I rowed on down the patch a ways and was going to start heading back toward shore. But I put a frog on, threw it back into this pocket in the rushes, and it no more than hit the water and there was a big swirl. The fish took off with my frog and I thought I had a big northern. I played it, in and out of the bulrushes, and worked it towards the boat. I couldn't believe it. Here was this bass with a mouth as big as a bucket. I was already excited, because I had those other bass, 5-1/2 and 6-1/2 pounds. This one made them look small!

I got it in the boat and headed for shore as fast as I could. Paul Nistler came out and asked me, "How did you do?"

I said, "You'll never believe it. Look at the size of this fish!"

Paul was all excited. We took it to several places in town for weighing, like Merlin Cox's grocery store and the Super Valu store. It weighed the same wherever we went, right around 8-1/2 pounds. Stan Razor, from the Litchfield newspaper, took pictures. And I entered it in as many contests as possible. I won the St. Paul *Dispatch-Pioneer Press* contest, bass division, and got "best in the state" for that year from *Sports Afield*. I won Stu and Dee Mann's contest, too.

That bass fishing on Lake Ripley is what really got me going on bass. Before that I fished a little of everything. Of course, you don't always get such big bass. Between 1968 and 1979 very few big bass were taken in that lake. Then, all of a sudden, in 1979 the big ones were there again. On my guiding trips that year we took 23 large-mouths over five pounds from Ripley, mostly in September and October. We threw all of them back except eight which were kept for mounting. Some were caught on spinnerbaits, but most of 'em hit frogs.

That frog fishing is quite a sport. When a big bass hits a frog it just about tears the rod out of your hand. The line takes off over the bulrushes. You're into and out of the rushes. You lose fish. You break lines. I've broken 14-pound test line like nothin'. You get a good-sized bass in the bulrushes and you've got your hands full!

A year or two after I caught that 8-1/2-pound largemouth, I was out on Ripley fishing for crappies, in spring before the bass season opened. It was around Mother's Day. I've seen crappies over two pounds come out of there, and bluegills up to a pound and a half.

So I was out there fishin' crappies, with crappie minnows and 4 or 6-pound line. There were a lot of boats out fishing, and the game warden from Litchfield was sitting on shore with his binoculars. While he was watching, I caught a bass that we figured went between 10 and 11 pounds! She was dripping with spawn. She was so full of spawn and slow in moving, I didn't have any trouble getting her in. She just sort of swam around like a big old log. I reached down, grabbed her by the lip and lifted her up.

A bunch of guys, including the warden, were standing on shore over by Nistler's boat landing. I quick rowed in there. The game warden said, "Let's measure it. I don't have a scale with me."

So we quickly measured the fish. It was 25-1/2 inches long. We put her back in the lake, and as far as I know she's still in there—unless she died of old age!

The Three Stooges at Manuella

It was around Labor Day, in September. I was walleye fishing with my father-in-law and my wife's uncle, Roy Hed, who used to be the business manager at the Litchfield school. Roy lacked the

Froggin' for bass in the reeds. Always that expectation of a lunker!

equipment and the experience, so he wasn't the best fisherman around. But he loved to fish.

We were on Lake Manuella, in the Dassel-Litchfield area. It was out from the south shore. She drops from five to about 22 feet, a gradual slope, and you'll find a couple little hooks along there. The break comes about a half a block from shore. It's sand bottom almost all the way in with a few sparse weeds and a little moss. Towards shore the bottom gets muddier with some lily pads scattered around. She's a good largemouth bass lake. Guys from Hutchinson's DNR office seine Manuella every year and they claim they've taken a walleye over 19 pounds, measuring 37 or 38 inches long. They're supposed to have caught it two years in a row.

Manuella, Stella, and Washington all run together, you know. A creek flows by the creamery on Stella and over towards Manuella. And there's a channel between Stella and Washington. I've seen walleyes in the 15 to 16 pound class being stripped by the state in that channel in spring. Lots of 'em in the 10-pound class. The year I caught my 8-1/2-pound largemough, 1968, Bud Rangeloff of Litchfield caught a 13-pound walleye on Washington. That's the biggest I ever heard of being taken around there by fishermen.

Then Manuella is fed by Sucker Creek which is a trout stream. So every once in awhile they'll catch a nice trout out of Manuella, but I've never heard of any trout coming from Stella or Washington. Of course, Manuella's deeper, it's spring fed, and it's got this creek coming into it. We never knew there were smallmouths in that lake, but we found out in a hurry on this walleye fishing trip.

It was just getting toward sundown. We were trolling with leeches, and we'd caught maybe half a dozen walleyes. Then, out of the clear blue, we got into a school of smallmouths, and I never saw such fast action in my life! Sometimes all three of us would have smallmouths on at the same time. It was just wild. We didn't know which one to net, because everybody was playing fish. The lines were going over each other and the fish were running every which way. And they were all fairly good-sized fish, from two to three pounds, good smallmouths! Fish were comin' in all over for a few minutes, and this Roy was giggling, laughing and hollering. We must have looked like the Three Stooges in that boat!

It only lasted about 10 or 15 minutes, but we must have caught about a dozen of those nice smallmouths. And during the time we tangled with those smallmouths we never caught a walleye.

Manuella is just one of many good fishing lakes in south-central Minnesota. In 1979 my 10-year old daughter caught a 3-1/2-pound smallmouth on Minnie Belle. We were fishin' on these scraggly cabbage weeds and she said, "I got a bite!" I said, "No, Dawn, I think you got weeds." She said, "This one ain't a weed, Dad!" And it sure wasn't!

There's Lake Erie, toward Hutchinson and south of Dassel, a good walleye lake. They catch a lot of walleyes there in spring and fall, plenty of 'em from shore. Belle's another good one. Most of these lakes have a variety of gamefish and panfish in them. Diamond Lake gets a big play on shore fishing.

Diamond's probably the best walleye lake around here. It's between Litchfield and Willmar, over by Atwater. I fish it quite a bit. One time I guided there for the Governor's Fishing Party on opening weekend. Dick Chapman from WCCO radio was with me, as was Ron Johnson of AAA's *Minnesota Motorist* magazine. We were about the only ones who caught fish on that occasion. We started out on the quiet side of the lake, like everyone else. All we got over there was some little bitty cigars. So I said, "Hey, let's go over and try that rough side."

The waves were rolling into the shallows there and the water was a little warmer. We just kept drifting back and forth, catching walleyes. We had a pretty good stringer when we came in but nothing big. All males, I s'pose. We had a lot of "keeper" size fish between 1-1/4 and 2 pounds. The guys who stayed on the quiet side didn't catch nothin'!

The Tail End of a Tornado at Green Lake

I got caught in a storm on Green Lake at Spicer and damn near died! I was fishin' with Chuck Hubbard. He guides up at Alexandria, but he used to live around Spicer.

Green is a big, deep lake. Every time you go out there you find new structure. The amount of bottom change in that lake is unbelievable! I fish Green a lot but it's hard to fish. About the time you think you've got a spot you might lose it and never find it again! It's up and down all over out there. I had a place where I caught two big smallmouths one night. One was 4-1/4 pounds, the other 4-1/2 pounds. It was on a kind of sand ledge that dropped from 17 to 22 feet. The fish were right on that ledge at 17 feet. I thought I had my bearings straight. I ran the graph over it. I ran the locator over it. But in the next 20 tries I couldn't find that spot!

Chuck and I were out on the lake this one night. I can't remember just what time of the year it was, but it must have been

Stan Nelson, guide in that Hutchinson-Litchfield-Spicer latitude.

in spring or early summer, the tornado season. It was towards evening and we were catching smallmouths on Lindy Rigs with leeches and crawlers. We were fishin' on a small bar near a bigger and more popular bar out towards the middle of the lake. We had a marker on the spot.

It was just as still and peaceful as could be, but it was clouding up and getting dark, like it might storm later on. We were fishing and shooting the breeze, the way fishermen do, not paying too much attention. Pretty soon I said to Chuck, "Listen to that darn train." He said, "They ain't got no trains around here!"

We looked over toward shore and here was the tail end of a tornado! The trees were just laying flat and branches were flying through the air. Here we are out in this bass boat, maybe two or three miles out in the lake. Green is maybe five miles across and there's hardly any protection. Chuck said, "Let's get that marker!"

I said, "The hell with that two-dollar marker! Let's get the heck out of here!"

I had a 65-horse Johnson on a Crestliner bass boat, that first bass boat Crestliner made, and we headed for the park at Spicer. We had launched at the ramp there and had to head into the wind to get back. By the time we got near shore we were fighting rollers probably seven feet high. They were huge.

The only thing that saved us was the fast action of guys on

141

shore. There must have been twenty of them, rescue guys from Spicer. I could see them trying to help others get in. I tried to hold my rig about a hundred feet from shore. I had that 65-horse outboard half wide open and we were sitting still! That's how hard the wind was blowing! The waves were coming into shore there at kind of an angle. I didn't think we'd drown, but I knew the boat could get smashed up in a wind like that.

So this one guy hollered at me. "Throw the keys! Throw the keys! Which car is yours?"

I pointed out which car was mine, threw them the keys, and they backed my boat trailer down the ramp. And I started heading the boat in there. Like I say, everything was flying around there—branches, leaves, and dirt. A couple boats got capsized out in the lake. But these guys were standing ready and they literally lifted my big bass boat out of the water and onto my trailer. They must have had eight or nine guys on each side of it. The waves were piling in there and throwing everything around. But the only damage was one little dent to the front of my boat.

I was never so scared in my life. When you hold a 65 half open and don't go no place, you know you've got wind! Outside of being scared, all we lost was that two-dollar marker.

We found out later that a tornado had gone through just a little ways north of us, maybe a half mile away, so we just caught the tail end of it. We were lucky. I never saw a storm come up that fast.

A New State Record Muskie —
19 Years After the Catch!

In January, 1976, I ended a *Fins & Feathers* magazine article with a plea for reliable information about certain record fish. One response came from Mark Windels, a columnist for Ed Gerchy's *Outdoor Outlines*. Mark suggested that I carefully check the 56-lb. 8-oz. Minnesota muskie record, caught on Lake of the Woods in 1931 by J. W. Collins of Baudette. He told me that Jimmy Robinson, the famed waterfowler and writer, insisted that this "record" was taken from Sabaskong Bay of Lake of the Woods—Ontario waters!

I failed to pursue the matter, but old Jimmy was serious and he brought his questions to the attention of Minnesota DNR officials and the press. The evidence was convincing. Minnesota suddenly had a new muskie record—a 54-pounder pulled from the fertile waters off High Banks on Lake Winnibigoshish one August afternoon in 1957. The new champ was Art Lyons, a retired Indian guide who had worked out of High Banks Resort.

The story of Art's new record hit the papers, but with few details. So I began a search for firsthand information. The old guide responded with some of the basics, then steered me to other sources: Bill Molzen, who operated High Banks Resort when Art hooked the big fish, along with retired Minneapolis policemen Don Hanson and George Ross, who were on the scene during the big muskie's fight with the Indian.

Following are stories and anecdotes pertaining to the 54-lb. muskie that was proclaimed a new state record in 1976, 19 years after it was caught.

Art Lyons and His Record Muskie
An Account of What Happened
As Told by George Ross

I was on the Minneapolis Police Department at the time. A friend of mine had a cabin up on federal land, about a mile or so away from High Banks Resort on Big Winnie. That was Don Hanson, another policeman. Don and his wife were good friends of Bill Molzen and his wife, the people who ran High Banks back then.

Anyway, we went up there for several days on a kind of vacation thing—Don and his wife Betty, my wife, Theresa, and myself. Don was still working on his cabin, but he knew that I liked to fish, so he suggested going fishing. The deal was we'd work a couple days and then go fishing.

It was late August, kind of a slow time, so Don said he'd go over to High Banks and talk to Molzen about getting Art Lyons to show us some fishing. We figured if Art wasn't busy he could take us out after northerns. It was just for the fun of it. The women liked to catch northerns. So we went over to High Banks, and Art had the time. It was in the afternoon. We took two boats out of there. Don and I and our wives were in one boat, with Don running the motor. And Art took the other boat by himself.

We worked back and forth along the High Banks area. Art said he'd try to locate the northerns for us. And he did. He'd catch a northern, or get strikes, and call us over. He'd say, "Try it here!"

I don't think we were ever much more than 30 yards from him. We just kind of trailed him, giving him casting distance.

Well, we must have been out a half hour or more, in a couple different spots. And he moved away from us a little bit more. We were getting a few strikes, nothing much. You know how four people can be in a boat, just gabbing and having a good time.

All of a sudden Art's not casting anymore. He was playing a fish, like he had hooked a good northern. He played it and played it. It would go down or out, like a northern would, and he didn't want to horse it. He just played it along. And this went on for awhile, maybe 15 or 20 minutes.

We had kept on fishing, and kind of watched Art work the fish. But pretty soon we stopped. We asked him what he had. And he said, "I think I might have hooked a good one," or something like that. We asked him how big he thought it was, and he said it might go 15 pounds. So we watched.

144

Guide Art Lyons with the 54-lb. muskie he caught out of High Banks Resort on Lake Winnibigoshish. The fish became a Minnesota record 19 years after the catch!

This went on for awhile and then the fish started moving more. Art would occasionally work the motor to keep his boat positioned right. We kind of kept out of the way because the fish was more on the move now. Sometimes it would stop. Then Art would stop and play with it some more. And I can remember hollering something like, "Art, I think you're kidding us. It looks like a little bigger one." He said, "Ya, I think it is a little bigger, maybe a 20-pounder!" sort of kidding us back.

Sometimes the weeds would just boil up. That fish would just tear 'em all up. But as this battle went on, Art and the fish kept working out away from shore, farther out in the lake. And we kept going out with them, in case Art needed help or something. The fish would fight and go down, and he couldn't do much with it. And then, after what must have been a good hour, or a little more, it started to come up more, toward the top. I can remember he kept on saying. "It's gonna come up. It's gonna come up."

Then he said it was coming up, and we got pretty close to him. He got it near the surface right in between the two boats. And, my God! None of us had seen anything like that. It looked like a piece of log! And you know how things look magnified in the water. The eyes! The head! And the length of it! The sight of that fish actually gave us a scary feeling. We were only a few feet from Art's boat, so the fish was right in front of us.

Then we decided to get more out of the way. And the fish went down again. About that time we realized that we had nothing to land it with. We had a little pike net, but that wasn't big enough. We didn't even want to try it. So Art told us about a gaff back at shore, one of those trap-like things with the jaws. With them you hit the fish and the jaws snap shut around it. So we went back to the resort to get it.

And everybody at High Banks knew something was going on because they could see us out there, just following Art around and not fishing. They were wondering what happened. We told 'em that Art had a hold of a pretty good-sized fish out there. They asked us about size and all kinds of questions, but we told them we just wanted the gaff.

We got the gaff and went back out there. He got the fish up again and tried the gaff, but it didn't close around that big fish. It snapped, but it bounced right off the fish. On second thought, it might have been Don who tried the gaff. Regardless, it didn't work. And down the fish went again.

Around this time we were getting out there, maybe a mile from shore. The lake was pretty quiet, but when the fish moved, it moved! Well, the gaff wouldn't work, so Don said he'd get in the boat with Art to help with the boat while he played the fish. And Art told me there was a big landing net on a launch, or some kind of boat, anchored out from the resort.

So I and the two women went in for that bigger net. We picked up the gal from High Banks Resort, Bill Molzen's wife, and she was all excited. She took us out to that steel launch to get the bigger net. Then she stayed in the boat with us when we took the net back to Art and Don.

The first time they used the net it wouldn't hold him. It was too small for that fish. But Art decided they'd get the head into the net, try to grab the fish, and just sort of flip it into the boat. And that's what they did. The fish was getting tired. Art told Don to get the fish's head into the net, and then he leaned over and grabbed it farther back and they hoisted it right into the boat. They worked together on the timing.

That fish really kicked around in the boat. Don had to sit on it. And we couldn't believe it! We raced back to shore with the two boats. I don't think Art is much more than five feet tall, and that fish seemed as long as Art! He had trouble holding it up but he did it. If I remember right, the fight with that fish took about an hour and a half, or an hour and forty-five minutes.

And then on shore people at the resort gathered to see it, and they horsed around for awhile. Pictures were taken and the fish was weighed. I think it weighed over 57 pounds at High Banks, like 57 pounds 6 ounces. So later on I was surprised to see it listed at 54 pounds. A few days after it was caught, they took Art's fish to Minneapolis for the Corrie's Contest. It was frozen then.

When he hooked that big muskie Art Lyons was using a medium sized red and white Dardevle, not the real small one and not the great big one. And somehow, when that fish first hit or maybe when it fought to shake the lure, it put a loop of line— like a half-hitch— around its head, just behind the gills. And when that line looped around there it got into the treble hook on the Dardevle. This loop pulled tight, around the fish, and maybe that's why the gills never cut the line. It was really something, I'll tell you!

When this thing came up about Art's fish being the record, I was glad to see him get some recognition. Because that little guy worked so hard with that big fish. I know he was thrilled. And we'll never forget it.

More on Art Lyons' 54-pound Muskie
As told by Don Hanson, retired Minneapolis policeman

While George Ross and our wives went in to get a big landing net Art and I battled the fish. We didn't have anything in Art's boat—no gaff and no net. All we could find was a short length of 3/4-inch pipe. I asked Art if I should hit the fish, and he said, "Yeah. Hit him!" So when Art got him up to the boat this one time I whacked him one across the snout. And even after it was mounted the fish showed a scar from where I hit him with that pipe.

I don't recall that the fish ever came completely out of the water. But when it rose to the surface and shook its head you could see that Art's line was full of weeds—from the reel clear down to the fish! It really stirred up the weeds.

After a half hour or so we ended up maybe 3/4 of a mile out in the lake from where Art first hooked the fish. Then the fish stayed pretty much down on the bottom, but once in a while Art would get him up. Art would get tired so I even took the pole. Art would

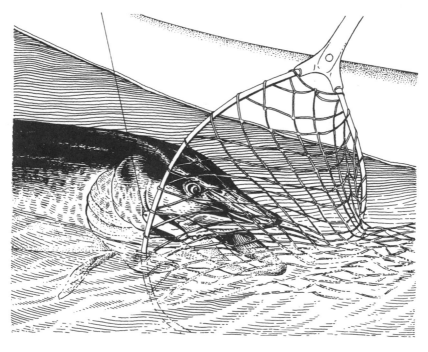

tell me to be careful, to thumb the line when the fish moved. But I soon gave it back to him. I got tired, too, and I didn't want to lose it for him!

Toward the end of the battle, after George got the bigger net, the fish finally started to move. And this time it came up to the top. Art kept working it back and forth until he got it near the boat. The first try with the net was in vain, because the fish went back down again. But the next time I took that northern pike net—with a hole in it—and pushed it over the front of the fish and we pulled it into the boat. Then I laid on top of it. By the time the fight was over we must have been a good mile and a half out in the lake. He had hooked it in that big weed bed that runs out from Tamarac Point.

The fish was first weighed in the boathouse out in front of the resort, by the dock at High Banks. I can't recall the weight, but I remember everybody being concerned about keeping the fish wet. They were afraid it would lose weight. Bill Molzen and Art were dead set on getting it to an official weighing station in Deer River before it lost a pound or two. They took off in a car, with the fish, and I remember Bill saying something about driving 90 miles an hour to get there. On the way back from Deer River they may have stopped in Bena to show the fish off.

It was a tremendous fish. I've got a big hand, and the space between that fish's eyes was bigger than the gap between my thumb and forefinger. That's why that pincher-type gaff wouldn't work. It wouldn't go over the fish's head!

Art Lyons was a typical good Indian guide, a nice fellow. He guided out of High Banks on a regular basis. They had a steel launch there, and it was his job to run it all summer. He knew the lake, and the woods too. He took me deer hunting a couple of times, and that son-of-a-gun could follow a track in the woods like nobody I've seen. It's amazing how that guy could read signs in the woods.

For a couple years in a row Art talked about seeing a big muskie. Nobody could say for sure that the one he caught was the same fish he saw. It was quite a coincidence, though, that he actually did catch this huge fish.

They froze the fish at High Banks and then some days later Bill Molzen took it to Minneapolis to enter it in Corrie's contest.

Author's note: The big muskie was caught on Wednesday, August 28, 1957. A picture of the fish, being held by resorter Bill

Molzen, was featured on the front page of the *Minneapolis Tribune* on Friday, August 30. The caption noted that the fish was "54 pounds heavy, 56 inches long."

According to the *Tribune* report, Molzen "brought the fish to Minneapolis for a sporting goods contest and told the tale of Lyons' luck." It said, "Lyons had taken a fishing party out on Big Winnie to show the anglers where to catch northerns. He made a few experimental casts with 20-pound test line and a red and white spoon. The monster hit. One hour and 48 minutes later, Lyons was able to bring the fish close enough to stun it with a piece of pipe."

Actually, as Don Hanson tells it, the pipe incident came earlier in the struggle. And it was Don, not Art Lyons, who whacked the muskie with the pipe.

The report goes on to say that Lyons' fish was "the largest taken in Minnesota for several seasons." But Minnesota Department of Natural Resources files list only one larger muskie, that 56 pound 8 ounce specimen from Lake of the Woods which was disqualified as the Minnesota record in 1976.

Retired resorter Bill Molzen told me he was the one who originally had the fish mounted. The trophy became his in return for taking it to Minneapolis for entry in the local contest at Corrie's Sporting Goods Store. Pete Hohn, a veteran *Minneapolis Tribune* photographer, took a shot of Bill and the muskie during that Minneapolis trip.

For many years Art Lyons' record muskie was on display in the bar at Bena, Minnesota, a notorious fishing town on Highway #2 at the south end of Lake Winnibigoshish. The mount had been reconditioned in the 1970's. In 1979 the bar building burned down, and the prize muskie was destroyed.

Charlie Janni, River Rat

When I talked fishing with Charlie Janni in December, 1979, he had been a resident of New Ulm for 84 years. The Minnesota River was young Charlie's playground, a source of income back in clam fishing days, and one of his favorite fishing scenes in later years. Charlie was well-known for his fishing and hunting exploits, and for his enthusiastic story telling.

Clam Fishin' on the Minnesota River

Clam fishin' was going strong on the Minnesota River around World War I time. It went on all along the river. Riverside Park in New Ulm looked like a town, a regular tent city! There were so many people from Iowa, and all over. They were after clamshells which got shipped to button factories. Most of ours went to Muscatine, Iowa.

We got those clamshells by the ton. By the carload! Hell, we had huge piles of 'em. They hauled 'em away with horse and wagon, and with trucks, too. At New Ulm, near Beyer's in Goosetown, there was always somebody loading clams on the sidetrack where the water tower and pump house were. They hauled 'em out in box cars!

I had been working in the harness shop downtown New Ulm, but I took off the whole summer of 1917 for clam fishin. Ole Gulden and Fergie (Adolph) Lampl owned the boats and clamming equipment. We worked for them. There was Shep (George) Grunnert, Joe Glaser, and myself. Joe Glaser didn't work too long. We spent most of the summer at Belview. But in August the river got so low we moved downstream toward New Ulm, above the KC Park at Henry Meyer's timber.

The boats were flat-bottomed, 20 feet long, with inboard engines. There'd be one guy to a boat. And each boat had two clam bars,

A mixed string, including dozens of slab crappies, from Big Stone Lake—where the Minnesota River begins—around 1900. (Minnesota Historical Society)

used one at a time. Those metal bars were 20 feet long, with strings and clam hooks hanging down—something like a trotline. Hooks were 4-pronged with no barbs. Later on we improved our rigs, linking the hooks with wire so we wouldn't lose so many.

The clams would be on the river bottom, open and facing the current, waiting to catch food as it washed downstream. As our hooks dragged along there those live clams would close on 'em. Usually if we caught a few clams there'd be more. They'd be standing thicker than heck! Then in some places there wouldn't be any and we'd have to go somewhere else.

We'd alternate with the two clam bars. While one was dragging out there we'd be picking clams off the other one. How many we got on a bar varied. Maybe there'd be 50, 75, 100, or more. And how long we dragged a bar depended on how thick the clams were. If we got a lot of clams we'd pull 'em out sooner.

As the boat moved downstream dragging the clam bar we were drifting with the current, not trolling with the motor. But we had

152

things set up with a rudder-like deal on the boat, so we could drift right or left as we wanted. You'd be surprised at how we could maneuver that boat—zig-zag or straight. We just used the motor to go back upstream for another drag through a clam bed. Maybe a bed would run for a block, or a half a block. They varied in size.

There were so many different kinds of clams. One was the lady finger. It was narrow and long, sort of bluish-pink. The buyers didn't want those. If you had too many of them in your pile you'd be docked, so we always threw them away. The best ones were the muckets and the pocketbooks. Then there was the three-ridge, about five inches in diameter. That was a big clam, and thick! Boy, they were heavy! The biggest clam was the pancake, but it was a little thinner. Another thin one was the paper shell. And there was the monkey face and the pimple back.

Maybe these different clams were right together, or maybe in their own separate places. It was hard to tell because you'd have all kinds on the bar. Of course, it wasn't so good if you went over a bed too often, because the clams would close up and it would take so long before they'd open again.

We didn't see many other clam fishermen at Belview, but there were two guys from Montevideo that fished there when we did. And there were two bums—nice guys, though—that fished around there. They were lazy and went out at maybe 9:30 or 10 in the morning and came in again around 2 in the afternoon. Hell, we put in long days! We'd have breakfast as soon as it got daylight and we'd work until dark. The more we fished the more money we made!

Old Gulden stayed on shore all the time. He cooked our meals and he also cooked the clams. We slept in a tent and we had a cook shanty. We had a metal cooker, maybe six feet long, and built a fire under it. We'd put the clams in there, boil 'em, and they'd open up. Next to the cooker we had a big work table where we'd shovel the meat out of the clams. That was a fast operation. The meat got pushed aside and the clamshell went on a pile.

We'd put that clam meat in barrels for farmers. It made good hog feed. We just wanted the shells. I remember when we were first up at Belview we didn't have a farmer to pick up the clam meat. So we dumped some of it in the river, right by the bank. And, boy, did the carp come in there! Sometimes at night there'd be hundreds of 'em! And you can believe this or not, but all their splashing washed out a big hole in the bank!

When I was a kid and that clam fishing was getting started

around New Ulm, we'd put a bunch of that clam meat in an old gunny sack, put a rock in there, and put it in the river. Then, usually in the evening, we'd take a boat out there and fish around it. The juices from that sack of clam meat got out into the river and brought in all kinds of fish. Boy, did we get the carp and catfish! We'd fish with fresh clam meat. In those days we had bamboo poles, without reels, and every once in awhile, bang! A big cat or something would hit and tear the whole line off!

Every once in awhile we'd catch something out of the ordinary. One time near Belview I came up with about 15 traps, muskrat traps. They were hangin' all over the clam bar. Either a fella lost a bunch of 'em, or maybe he drowned with a bunch of traps on him! They must have been in the water a long time because the springs were very weak. And one time I came up with a great big head that had short horns on it. We nailed it up on a tree where we camped. They always said, "That's a buffalo." It was real old.

When we clam fished at Belview we'd leave New Ulm with the boats in May, when the river was high. This one time we had two boats in front, with motors, pulling two other clam boats and a smaller boat behind. They were loaded down with all our camping gear, tents and all. We had the clam cooker on one of the boats. And I even had my dog and doghouse along!

When we got to Franklin we first wanted to stop on the south side of the river, below the bridge. There was a high bank along there that was still above water. But Fergie Lampl said, "Ach, we'll stop a little ways up from the bridge!" So we squeezed under the bridge and camped up above there. And it's a good thing we did, because that night the bridge went out. It tore loose from the opposite bank, swung around, and washed right into the high bank where we were first going to camp!

I remember we went across the river and laid branches and logs across the road so nobody would drive into the water.

Back when that clam fishing was a big thing there'd be people camping every so often along the river. At that time George Fesenmaier had a grocery store in New Ulm, and he ran a special grocery route for the clam fishermen. He'd go way up the river by motorboat, taking orders along the way. Then the next morning he'd be out delivering groceries and taking more orders.

Gulden and Lampl paid us by the big candy pail full. And they sold the clamshells by the ton. Buyers would come around. One buyer's name was VanShake, or something like that. He was kind of a complainer. One time when we were cooking clams I found a pearl, a real dandy. And he wanted to buy it for $25. I told him, "Oh, no!" I had it put in a ring for my wife.

There were a few people that fished clams pretty early. There was a fella by the name of Schmidt, from Fairmont, who had a tent by the river. He fished close to New Ulm, near Bartl's and Fritsche's. That must have been back around 1908. There was still some clam fishing going on later, maybe in the early 1920's. I know after a while Otto Schneider from New Ulm bought clams. He was also in the fur business.

There were no limits on what we could take, but later on we had to have a license. And finally they closed clam fishing altogether because they got less and less.

Fishing Walleyes at Reim's Camp

I fished walleyes a lot at night on the Minnesota River, especially at Reim's Camp, upstream from New Ulm. I had a boat up there and I'd drive up there about 4 or 5 o'clock in the afternoon. There used to be a big tree layin' in the river, with big dry branches stickin' out. They made kind of a big crotch. I'd run my boat in there and tie it to the tree. That's where I'd fish for walleyes and catfish.

When there was a full moon, when the moon came up over Hartman's place, you could see the bobbers so nice. I remember one time I was there, fishin' with frogs. I'd keep the frogs in a box I made, with a baggy canvas top that had a zipper on it. With a flat or tight cover the frogs would jump out, but with this cover they'd just hit that loose canvas and stay inside. Well, I had that box right next to me in the boat, I was fishin' with two poles.

I had a few walleyes already. Then I caught one that weighed maybe three or four pounds. At the same time I had a bite on the other pole, so I quick took that fish off, laid him down, and grabbed the other pole. Here I had laid that fish on the frog box and that son-of-a-gun jumped over the side of the boat and back into the river!

Not too far from that place, right across the river from Reim's, there was a great big cottonwood tree. Ooh, he was a monster! It had broken off, or the river washed it out, and it fell in—stickin' out in the river. Brush and junk would come floatin' along and build up around that tree. The trash got so thick in there by fall that it was solid, kind of mossy, and grass growing on it. And a big log came to rest against that stuff.

My wife and I would take the boat, go around behind it, and leave it there. Then we'd get out on that stuff and fish. We'd be sittin' pret' near out in the middle of the river! We'd fish with long bamboo poles with reels on them. I'd lay my poles on that log. At first, whenever I got a bite the pole would slip and fall off of there. So one day I brought two spikes to pound in there about an inch apart, and then I laid my pole in between 'em. Then it couldn't slip away. We'd get walleyes and cats that way.

And I had a fly rod that I'd use for crappies there. Every once in awhile one would come out of that brush pile. Bing! And the fly rod bent over.

We fished there for two years and then one spring the whole works was gone. That was one of the best fishing spots I ever had.

Trotlines in the River

We had trotlines in the river when I was a kid, and even later. Everybody had 'em. We'd tie the line on one side and run it almost all the way across the river. On the end in the river we'd have a heavy weight to hold the line down. There was that main rope going across the river, with separate cords or leaders, maybe 12 or 15 inches long, going down to the hooks. One trotline might have as high as 200 or 250 hooks on it!

If you had the hooks too close together fish might tangle together. Sometimes hooks would be gone or the line all twisted up. Catfish would do that. They'd get caught and then roll and twist. Later on, the guys who could afford it used swivels on those drop-leaders to prevent that twisting.

When we were kids we'd go out to check the crossline for the last time as it was getting dark. And the mosquitos! We fished with worms, baited all those hooks with worms. Your hands would be dirty and slimy from those worms, and then you'd hit your face—here, there, and all over. We'd get all smeared up. The kids looked like mud piles!

We'd get big fish, too. I caught a sturgeon that weighed 53 pounds, and a 40-pounder. That was back in 1906, '07, and '08, when I was 12 and 13 years old. 10- and 20-pound rubbernose sturgeon were common at that time. We'd catch a lot of carp, catfish, sheepshead, and sturgeon, but not many walleyes, and not many bullheads either. I don't know why. And we didn't get many buffaloes, but the river was loaded with them. On the hooks near

shore, on the drop-off, we'd hang frogs and catch northerns. We called 'em pickerel at that time.

My biggest catfish was caught on a trotline when I was working already, maybe around 1915 or 1916. I remember I cut myself in the shop and had my hand all bandaged up. I went out to the river one night to check my crossline and there was that big catfish. I knew darn well I couldn't handle him, so I dropped it back in the water and went back to town for my spear. Then I speared him— with only one prong! It was so dark.

157

That fish weighed 32 pounds and I sold it to Charlie Manderfeld. He was in the saloon business on Broadway, next to Hubby Zupfer's barbershop in New Ulm. He gave me two bucks for it, and that was a lot of money.

And one time when I was just a kid I got a big northern. I had him in a gunny sack. I couldn't really carry that fish on my bicycle, so I tied him over the handle bars and pushed the bike. I wanted to take it up to the light plant where my dad was a fireman. There was an engineer there who stayed at the old Merchant Hotel. He always said if I got a big fish he wanted it.

But I didn't get as far as the light plant. When I passed the Great Northern depot, Richard Pfefferly came out. He was a telegrapher. And he said, "By God! You've got a big fish in there! What is it?"

I told him it was a pickerel. And he said, "What do you want for it?"

I said, "What'll you give me?"

He said, "Seventy-five cents."

"It's yours!" I said. It was probably a 20-pound northern!

I was excited with that money. I got on that bike and was home in two minutes! Mother asked me, "What happened?"

I told her, "I sold it! I got seventy-five cents! Look here, ma!"

Gene Shapinski, Unorthodox Angler

As a fishing expert, Gene Shapinski's credentials are impressive enough: Tackle shop operator and outdoor writer in South Bend, Indiana; promoter for Cisco Kid lures; fishing guide from 1951 into the late 1960's in the Brainerd, Minnesota area; maker of spectacular fishing films; inventor and maker of Gene Shapinski's Quiver Jig; and angler extraordinaire.

A Deal with Towner
Trading Fish for Meat

Long before we settled in the Gull Lake area in 1951, Marge and I spent lots of time fishing in Minnesota. One summer we stayed at Gull and ran into a guy with whom we traded walleyes for meat! I think it was right after World War II and for some reason it was hard to buy meat. All you could buy around there was cold meat and chicken no pork chops!

The fella's name was Towner, and he had a big supermarket in Rochester. He was going to the Mayo Clinic there and the doctors told him he was overworked, and that he should take a vacation. That's how we happened to meet him, fishing at Gull Lake.

Anyway, this Towner couldn't catch any fish. But he loved to eat walleyes. So I did some thinking and told Marge I was gonna have a talk with him. I went up to him and I said, "Mr. Towner, my name is Gene Shapinski. I understand you have a supermarket down in Rochester."

He said, "Yes."

I said, "I tell you what I'll do. I'll make a deal with you. I'll get you the walleyes and exchange them for some meat, like pork chops, ham, and beef."

He looked at me and said, "How do you know you're gonna get the walleyes?"

I said, "Don't worry about that. I'll catch the walleyes!"

He said, "Okay. I've got confidence in you. I'm gonna make a long distance call right away. I'll order the meat now, before you go fishing."

He made that call and told them to pack pork chops, ham, beef, and steaks. He really sent us a bunch of meat. Now I had my work cut out for me.

So next day Marge and I went out and came back with a stringer of Gull Lake walleyes you could hardly carry. The limit was eight back then, so we came in with 16 good-sized walleyes. We caught 'em on Cisco Kids and Pikie Minnows in the weeds, in shallow water. This was in spring.

I'd go deeper in July and August, but still near the edge of the weeds. In all the years I guided on Gull I seldom fished deeper than 15 feet for walleyes. In fact, I can remember the lake being just green with bloom, in the heat of summer, and we'd catch those walleyes right up in the weeds. And you couldn't see three feet through that green water.

Anyway, Marge and I got our meat and Towner got his walleyes!

Catching a Northern Pike on Another Northern

Jerry Carnes had an outdoor show on KSTP Television in the Twin Cities. I was on that show several times. On one show I had a big northern with me. That fish weighed about 20 pounds and there's an interesting story behind it.

It happened on Sylvan Lake, near Gull Lake. I was fishing for northerns with a guy from South Bend, Indiana. I was using a muskie-size Cisco Kid lure—really a muskie lure, but I liked it for northerns.

I hooked onto a northern that weighed about two pounds. Sylvan Lake was clear so I could see some distance through the water. As I was bringing in this fish I saw a big shadow or dark form approaching the small northern I had hooked. All of a sudden a big northern had a hold of my smaller fish, which was hooked on the Cisco Kid!

I told Walter—that was the guy's name—that another northern had a hold of the northern I was bringing in. Well, the fish—or should I say the two fish?—started swimming off to one side. So I gave him line. Well, he got into the weeds and stopped, hopefully to

160

swallow the smaller northern. That was my only chance for hooking the big northern.

I waited. Walter said to me, "Holy smokes! It must be twenty minutes!"

It really was about ten minutes, I think, but he was getting impatient. I didn't care, though, I waited another five minutes. I figured I better set the hook hard, so that if the lure's hooks were anywhere near the big one's mouth I'd stand a chance of getting 'em sunk in. So I really reared back and my tubular steel rod exploded in my hand—busted! I started reeling in without the benefit of a bending rod, with the broken part sliding on the line! I worked the fish out of the weeds and finally landed it. I believe it was close to 20 pounds.

Anyway, Jerry Carnes had it mounted—the big northern, the smaller northern sticking out of its mouth, and the Cisco Kid lure that started the action. Probably should have mounted the broken rod along with it!

Meyer Lake Northern Hits Bass and Runs

One time I was fishing for largemouth bass on Meyer Lake, a little lake near Crosslake, Minnesota. I hooked a bass which I judged to weigh about three pounds. I saw it when it jumped out of the water the first time. While it was in the air a second time, a huge northern came up and smacked it—right before my eyes!

That time everything flew—the northern, the bass, and my lure. The line broke and I lost the whole works. That was really something to see. All that unexpected excitement and commotion on the water. Then nothing!

A Pack of "Wolves" in Wolf Lake?

This took place years ago. My brother Stan and I were fishing for bass on Wolf Lake, near Andrusia and Cass Lakes. It was early summer and we were fishing near where Andrusia connects with Wolf. There were some lily pads there, inside the edge of a deep drop-off. It dropped maybe eight or 10 feet right out from the pads.

We were using Creek Chub plunkers. I thought the Creek Chub was the only plunker that would really work. To me, the others were poor imitations. This lure was deadly when fished on the surface for bass, if it was worked right! There was a certain correct action that would make all the difference.

162

After retiring from guiding, Gene Shapinski became a panfish expert.

Well, I cast my plunker and dropped it right next to the pads. Just as I started working it I could see the lily pads sort of weaving—like something big was moving through them. All of a sudden, bang! I set the hook and just like that the plunker was gone.

I'll make the story short. I had seven plunkers in my tackle box. We were rigged with 12-pound line for bass. What happened was that my brother and I fed all those plunkers to big muskies. Some came out of the water near the boat so I could see them. I know some were pushing 30 pounds.

Were there seven different muskies? Or just a couple savage ones? I don't know. I do know that those lily pads seemed alive. There had to be fish down there to move around those pads, which weren't all that close together. After that experience we often remarked that we must have tangled with a pack of wolves in Wolf Lake!

18-pound Northern Jumps into Boat

It happened on Big Hubert Lake, in the summertime. Steve Davis was along with me. Steve was from La Grange, Illinois, and was about 12 years old at the time.

There was hardly any wind blowing. It was an ideal day for surface lures. We were fishing a surface lure called The Darter, the Creek Chub Darter. It was yellow, with orange dots. We were in about 12 to 15 feet of water, with a very rich growth of cabbage weeds below us.

Steve was in the middle of a retrieve when I suggested, "Steve, throw over that way." So he speeded up his retrieve, eager to cast where I told him to. About that time, as he quickly chugged the lure toward the boat, this huge northern came out of the water—cleared the water by at least three feet—and landed right in the center of the boat!

The northern flopped like crazy on the bottom of the boat. And Steve was flabbergasted. He quickly jumped on the fish and tried to hold him down. He shouted, "I caught a muskie! I caught a muskie!"

Of course it was a northern. And he never touched the lure! The fish weighed 18 pounds. The picture and story appeared in the *Brainerd Dispatch*.

Art Barneveld, Launch Skipper

Art Barneveld began his Mille Lacs Lake launch fishing career rather suddenly in the late 1940's. "The first time I ever took a launch out was when my older brother, Barney, made a trip to Rhode Island. He had a bunch of reservations and said, 'You take 'em fishin'!'—just like that! Before that Barney did the fishin' and I did the farmin'."

After that they both did the fishin', day after day, summer after summer. At the time of this writing Art was gearing up for another Mille Lacs season.

Flatfish 'n' Worm Days

Flatfish fishing was going strong back in the early 1950's. Wyman Johnson, another Mille Lacs launch pilot, had the big YOBHY (You Oughtta Been Here Yesterday) at that time. I can still see him running around on that big boat with Flatfish lines flyin' all over. It seemed the more Flatfish you had out the better the luck for everybody. We tried it both ways. When we had 10 Flatfish out everybody caught more fish than when we had four or five in the lake. More Flatfish meant more walleyes per person.

The usual Flatfish sizes were the X4 and X5, with one treble hook on the rear and two small trebles in the middle. Right from the start we took those middle hooks out because they'd foul up the landing net, and make the usual line tangles worse. And without those middle hooks the action was better. The lure would wobble more. When fishing was extra good you'd get fish on plain Flatfish. But most of the time we'd hang a nightcrawler or a gob of angle worms on the rear treble.

Those X4 and X5 models were pretty small, about three inches long. But later on they came out with the big U20, with four hooks on it—two trebles in the middle and two on the rear. We'd load up every hook with a bunch of worms. I've seen some big fish caught on them!

There were some funny things with those Flatfish. We'd buy 'em six to the carton. You could throw six new ones out there and maybe have two out of those six that would catch fish! The other four were just for looks. I don't know what the difference was.

At first we used nothing but orange ones with black spots. Then the orange with a black stripe got hot. Later it was yellow, silver, and every color you could think of. But there were Flatfish that worked and Flatfish that didn't. And about the time they shifted from wood to plastic it sort of went downhill.

Flatfish fishing got good in late spring when the water warmed up. We'd start with minnows early in the season and then switch over to Flatfish 'n' worms, especially around the time the walleyes moved out to the mud flats.

The biggest killing I ever made was on Flatfish. We had 92 walleyes on a morning launch trip by 11 o'clock. It was a dead calm morning in July, a good mud flat fishin' day. The gnats were thicker than hell, and the fish were bitin' like damn fools! I never put a line in the water for myself until 10 o'clock. I was just too busy scoopin' fish, puttin' worms on Flatfish, and stringin' fish. There'd be 10 or 15 walleyes layin' in the boat before you'd get a chance to string 'em. There were fish comin' in all the time—all

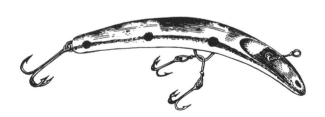

The Flatfish

Invented in 1933 by Detroit auto worker Charles Helin, a bass fishing enthusiast. He founded the Helin Tackle Co. in 1937.

sizes. We finally ran out of worms, but they'd bite just as good on the bare Flatfish.

It didn't seem to matter where you fished that morning. I thought I was smart going over to this one flat. But shortly after I headed in Barney was goin' in too, loaded up with fish from another spot.

We had a lot of good Flatfish trips. I remember one session in an area a few miles out in the lake. The bottom there is a series of humps and dips. You might have a hump of mud about as big as a house, where the bottom comes up to 20 or 22 feet and then goes back down to 28. Go a little ways and there's another hump like that, and some more. She'll come right up and go back down— hardly a boat length across the top!

There was a guy from Iowa. McQueen was his name. There were five or six in his party that time. They pulled in here late, after three in the afternoon. I had to take 'em fishing. Well, we didn't do much until we got out to those humps and hollows, maybe around 5 o'clock. All at once all hell broke loose. We were in the big walleyes.

McQueen was always talkin'. They had to be 19 inches long or else they weren't fit to keep. And they had to be 19 inches to collect the jackpot money, too. We had 'em 19 all right, but some of 'em on that trip got pretty close to 30 inches long!

That McQueen was a great one for using big old U20 Flatfish. And he left all the hooks on it, too. Gol damn fish trap! He even managed to snag one walleye in the back!

It was generally Flatfish with worms. But I've seen 'em hang everything on Flatfish. One time I had a bunch out from Land O' Lakes. This one guy was too looped up or too lazy to hang a worm on. So he hung on a piece of smoked turkey skin and came up with a 7-pound walleye. So everybody on the boat was lookin' for smoked turkey rind! Other times I caught a lot of fish with little frogs hangin' on there.

And you could get tangled with those Flatfish! On the launches we'd just cut 'em off, save the hardware, and start over. We'd hang out 10 or 12 lines on the old 30-foot launches. Sometimes a big walleye would go around and take in a bunch of Flatfish on the way up. What a mess!

Here's a good Flatfish story. Back around '55 or '56, Alice DePew was draggin' a Flatfish behind the launch. She got a big fish on. And while she cranked it in she poked the rod butt into her belly, like a lot of people do. The harder the walleye pulled the harder she poked herself. And when we got her fish in the boat she hollered, "Oh, my God! My incision!" That's all she said.

It didn't dawn on me at first. But then I remembered. About two weeks earlier she had surgery for appendicitis. And there she was, poking the fishing rod into her stomach! It didn't go through, but it hurt I s'pose. She was too darn excited about her big fish to know if it hurt or not!

A Wallet on Ice

It was a nice warm day. I had this bunch out fishin' with me in the morning. They were half loaded then already, but we went out again in the afternoon.

This one guy had been fishing up in the front end of the launch. But then he went back to see his partner. I heard some noise or scufflin' and turned around. I don't know what went on. I looked and all I seen was his feet goin' over the edge of the boat!

In about two steps I was back there. He came up about that time, so I grabbed him by the hair, and his buddy grabbed him by the arm, and we flipped him back in the boat.

Then I looked over the edge and saw his billfold floatin' in the water. It was too far away to net, so I got back to the wheel and turned the boat around. I told this other guy up in the front end, "His billfold is floatin' over there. Scoop it up if it's still on top when I get by it."

So I got by it and he scooped it up in the net. Meanwhile, the guy that fell in is wipin' his glasses off and settling down. He gets his glasses back on, feels his pockets, and says, "Oh, my God. My billfold. A hundred and twenty dollars gone to hell!" And so on.

Meantime, the guy who scooped it out of the lake threw the billfold into a cooler in the front of the boat. After the guy who fell in simmered down and decided he lost everything, he thought he might as well have another beer. So he opened the cooler and there was his wallet. He shouted, "Hell, I never lost my billfold. Here it is, still in the cooler!"

That's how bad off he was. He never knew his wallet was in the lake!

Poundage

Over the years we've had tremendous catches of walleyes. But one trip stands out. And it wasn't so long ago, in the 1970's. The

168

Mille Lacs Lake launch skipper Art Barneveld (left) with chunky walleye.
(Photo by Milton Rosko, Jr.)

smallest was a solid two pounds, but we had lots of big ones, up to eight pounds. The wind must have been out of the northwest, because I can remember buckin' the waves on the way home.

There was Charlie Wawa the hat salesman, Jack Olson, and old Tony—I guess I had maybe eight or nine people on the boat. Charlie and them always fished afternoons. Oh, we were into lunkers this one afternoon! Jack had his six walleyes and they weighed 36 pounds. He had fished Mille Lacs for 40 years and that was the first time he ever came up with anything like that.

This was pretty far out in the lake, on a small mud flat. It's a small hump that I like to haunt because I can catch a few big ones there. It's worked lots of times. It's maybe a block long at the most, and half of that wide. She just goes plunk on the east side, right straight down. But, God, they were in there that one time. We really lit into 'em.

Everybody on the boat was usin' minnows and spinners, and we filled out. They had the limit by about 5 o'clock. That was the biggest load of fish, poundage, that I ever had on my launch.

Jerry Fuller of Park Rapids

Jerry Fuller is a son of the late Earl Fuller who made his family's name prominent in retail and wholesale tackle businesses.

Fuller's, and the Longest Running Fishing Contest in Minnesota

The Fullers got their start in Park Rapids with my grandfather, Frank Fuller, who came to town in 1883 and set up a hardware business on Main Street. Frank Fuller was from Rothsay, Minnesota. When he died in 1912 the business was still strictly a hardware store with very little in the way of sporting goods. But my dad, Earl Fuller, took it over that year and began emphasizing the sporting goods more and more.

Over the years we've had several locations in Park Rapids. The business burned to the ground in 1928, or thereabouts, and when we opened a new store, about 1930, sporting goods was the big thing. Also in 1930, we opened a sporting goods store in Grand Rapids and maintained it until 1960. It later became Rapids Tackle. The present Fuller's Tackle Shop in Park Rapids was built in 1970.

Fuller's wholesale tackle business began back during World War II time. My mother ran the store while my dad took the truck out and resold at a marginal discount to resorters and bait shops. In 1949 we built the wholesale building and hired others to drive trucks.

Fuller's fishing contest was begun by my dad, Earl, at the start of the fishing season in May, 1915, when Fuller's was still a hardware store. That first year they gave out prizes for largemouth bass only. Then in 1916 they went to northerns, walleyes, muskies, and panfish. This is surely the longest running fishing contest in Minnesota. And I believe it is the longest running fishing contest in the United States, with the exception of Field and Stream's, which began shortly before Fuller's.

Traditionally, area businesses put up the weekly prizes for each species of fish. And the resorts have furnished the prizes for season

Mr. and Mrs. Earl Fuller in front of their Park Rapids Tackle Shop in 1946. Fuller's Tackle grew out of Fuller's Hardware, established in the 1880's by Earl's father, Frank.

winners. We've tried to push lots of smaller prizes rather than one big prize, a policy which results in many winners. The pros are kept out of the contest. And the fish must be caught in our contest area—lakes and streams around Park Rapids. We operated a separate contest, with the same format, out of our Grand Rapids store.

The Golden Book and Fishing Directory, listing contest entries and winners, as well as other fishing information, dates back to 1916. We had the Blue Book at Grand Rapids during the many years of that contest.

The Minnesota DNR took several decades of the Golden Books and contest records to determine trends. Don Olson, fisheries biologist from Detroit Lakes, worked on that project. Don and his co-workers charted, graphed, and computed the figures every way imaginable.

Their work showed muskies and northern pike fishing peaking out in the early 1940's. Shortly after World War II there was a sharp decline in the average size of those fish. Muskies really dwindled, while northern pike maintained their numbers but dropped in size.

On the other hand, in the "good old days" of the late 1910's, 1920's, and early 1930's, a 6-1/2-pound walleye was really something. Now we get many more big walleyes. In 1978 an 8-pounder wouldn't even place. A 12-pounder won the contest. The large-mouth bass entered in our contest have also increased in weight over the years. In the 1970's our season winners have been over 7 pounds. Forty and 50 years ago the largemouth winners would be around 6 or 6-1/2 pounds, or even less.

So bass have basically held their own, and that's true of the panfish as well. In fact, we have probably received more big blue-gills recently than in many years past. Part of that may be due to increased attention toward that species, rather than to a change in fish populations. That more people fish bass in deep water may be a reason for more big bass.

Contest Cheating
A "Clank" on the Scale!

Over the years, we've seen all kinds of things in the bellies of fish entered in our contests—like beer cans filled with sand, and sinkers. The most notable instance of cheating, at least in my memory, involved a really fine northern pike. As it turned out, that fish would have honestly won the season's second place northern pike prize. Without the added weight it would have been a close second.

We keep no padding on the scales, so fish aren't supposed to go clank when they're weighed. But we threw this northern on there and heard a definite clank. So we took it into the back room and milked two fist-sized rocks out of its belly. They had added 11 ounces to the fish, enough to get it into first place! Of course, those rocks disqualified the entry.

That fish was brought in by a resort owner's son. And he just couldn't imagine how that northern picked up those rocks. He tried to infer that it probably was like a chicken picking up gravel to help its digestion! We didn't quite go along with that.

A Trophy Belle Taine Smallmouth

One of the biggest smallmouth bass ever to come out of the Park Rapids area was brought into Fuller's from Lake Belle Taine in 1976 or 1977. Belle Taine is at the bottom end of the Mantrap Chain. That whole chain of lakes has smallmouth in it.

This guy's fish weighed 6 lb. 15 oz. That was a really big smallmouth for this area, because season winners are usually in that 5-1/2 to 5-3/4 pound range. It's the biggest smallmouth I can remember.

The interesting thing about this catch is that the fellow who caught it didn't know what kind of fish he had! He thought it had "funny spots" on it, "gray patches." He wanted to know if it was any good to eat!

Most of the serious smallmouth fishermen would give their left arm, and maybe part of the right arm, for a fish that big. But this guy didn't know what a smallmouth looked like. Needless to say, he was quite pleased to find out that he had caught a really good fish.

Big Browns from the Straight River and Straight Lake

The biggest trout from around Park Rapids was a 14-lb. 15-oz. brown, the second biggest I know of from Minnesota. That came from Straight Lake in the winter time.

We have a mount of an 8-lb. 14-oz. brown trout, the biggest

174

brown I know of that was legally caught from the Straight River. It was caught by a woman who was fishing with a Strip-on spinner and a dead minnow.

Her husband had left her in the car at the 7-mile bridge while he worked up and down the stream with his waders and more appropriate gear. The wife got bored in their car and decided to fish. She took that nice puppy of a trout right out from under the bridge, using that hunk of hardware!

Fuller's Guides, Including Sy Siebert

When I was a kid guiding was different from what it is now. We had Fuller's Guides, basically all the good fishermen around town that were available for guiding tourists in summer. Sometimes my dad would have to round 'em up and get them sober if they had a job the next day!

They had sheriff's type badges. And I remember that old Sy Siebert was Fuller's Guide No. 1. Sy was a colorful fisherman who was on the scene here for years and years. Stories about Sy are legion. He was not a complete stranger to the truth, and he certainly was no stranger to whiskey. He was an interesting, classical type fellow who knew a lot about fish. And he knew plenty about human nature. He could talk up his guiding efforts and come back with a better buck than anybody else at that time.

He'd stand out in front of the store, by the display window with the fish on ice, and tout his guiding prowess. He'd ask, "What kind of fish do you want to catch?"

Or he'd say, "I was guiding that fella who caught this big fish. Would you like to catch one like it? Double or nothin' if we do?"

And Sy had a log in Big Mantrap Lake. He'd set the people up and tell them, "This is the home of the old tiger. Get ready. He's just around the corner."

They'd get hung up on his log, and sometimes he'd "accidentally" run the motor the wrong way and help break their lines. Sy was a real character and quite a guide.

A Fish Hook Lake Northern that Never Made it to Town

Back in the wooden rowboat era when I was quite young, a friend of mine, Eddy Andersen, and I were out on Fish Hook Lake

176

casting for northerns. There was another fellow out there, a vacationer, who was also casting for northerns. We watched that guy boat a pretty nice fish, but he never made it to town with it.

He was using a deep-sea type outfit. And he hooked this big northern right near the boat. He winched the big fish in, gave a holler, and it was in the boat in about one second flat. He reefed it right in!

We were close enough to see the fish go over the gunwhale and into the boat. It was big! As soon as that fish got in the boat, the middle seat flew up in the air in about six pieces! It looked like shrapnel! Whether the fish broke it or the guy fell on it, I don't know. The sequence of events was just too much. Eddy and I were at that wiseacre age of 15 or 16 and didn't do a thing to help. We convulsed with laughter.

The fish apparently got off the hook while it thrashed around the guy's boat. He was stomping around and trying to hit it with an oar. He dropped his rod. And suddenly, in the middle of it all, the fish did a flip-flop out of the boat!

Jim Heddon
Spurning Outboard Motors and Live Bait

Years ago, Jim Heddon had a cabin on Long Lake, just three miles east of Park Rapids. Jim was the original Heddon of bait company fame. Several of his early Heddon lures were developed on Long Lake. The Heddons had that cabin from the 1910's until old Jim died, maybe in the early 1940's.

He spurned outboard motors. And he had little time for anybody using live bait. He was putting his money where his mouth was. Jim was selling artificial plugs and that's all he used for bass.

My dad and Jim Heddon got along okay. Jim was a tournament caster and my dad was a big buff on that. And dad didn't fish with live frogs, because he didn't sell them. But the old Heddon wouldn't communicate with a couple of the local guides because he saw them fishing with frogs. And he wouldn't swap bass fishing stories with them. He was a good guy, but an independent character!

Minnesota TV Fishing 1950's Style

With fishing claiming more participants than does any other Minnesota sport, TV fishing shows win large audiences in the Gopher State. Two of my all-time favorites date back to the 1950's when television and I were both growing up.

Rollie Johnson's "Hunting and Fishing" and Stu Mann's "Minnesota Outdoors" were pioneer outdoor shows which few of the old viewers will ever forget. What a novelty it was to have colorful hosts like Rollie and Stu bring fishing from the land of sky-blue waters into the local angler's living room!

Here, these broadcasting veterans reflect on their old shows and offer a couple favorite fishing stories.

Stu Mann's "Minnesota Outdoors," As Stu Remembers

When I was a sportscaster with WLOL in the late 1940's, I met the chap who got me interested in the outdoor program idea. He was a fella by the name of Cal Johnson, who at that time held the world record muskie catch from near Hayward, Wisconsin. Cal was a famous outdoor writer who also did some work for a Chicago radio station. Anyway, he and I got together for a radio show on WLOL. And in the years that followed we fished together often, especially at Teal Lake in Wisconsin where we caught lots of crappies.

It was around 1949 or 1950 that we put together a radio outdoor show called "The Sportsman's Roundtable," first heard on WLOL radio. It consisted of a colorful panel, including Tony Lane, an archery expert; Roger Preuss, a wildlife authority and artist; "Uncle Ed" Franey, a trout fishing buff and outdoor writer for the old *Minneapolis Times*; Cap Lund, known as Mr. Ducks Unlimited; and Cliff Sakry, a key man in rejuvenating the Minnesota Conservation Federation. These were all great outdoorsmen and good fishermen.

The program moved to WTCN radio and then, in about 1954, to WTCN-TV. That same great panel made the moves with me. Actually, the show was organized with television in mind. I went to WTCN television, then in the Calhoun Beach Hotel, and presented the idea to them. They liked it. The show ran for eight years, winning three national awards, all signed by Walt Disney.

Each week we'd have a panel discussion on an outdoor topic. We had guest panelists and often showed fishing and hunting films. In the last part of the show we'd field questions sent in by the viewing audience. The mail was terrific!

Some of our guests were fishing guides. They'd often be on the films we shot during fishing trips, films we'd run while they were on the show. And we had guests like Thorny Pope of Pope's sporting goods store in Minneapolis. He was a terrific fisherman and visited the show quite a few times. So did Dr. George Selke when he was Department of Conservation Commissioner. And then there was Jake Pete from Ely, one of the most colorful outdoorsmen I've ever known. We made movies with him and his cabin boat operation up on Basswood Lake. It was through our show that TV star Joan Davis got lined up for a week of fishing and relaxing on one of Jake's cabin boats. After seeing one of our shows, her dad contacted us and we made the arrangements with Jake. We even sent our cameramen up there to take movies of Joan, but the film became lost when we loaned it to a pretty red-headed singer at Mr. Nib's, a night spot in Minneapolis.

The panel had many interesting debates. We'd tackle questions like year-round fishing for members of the sunfish family. Back in the old days, remember, crappie and bluegill fishing ended on February 15 and didn't start again until the walleye season opener in May. We were against that. We felt these panfish should be fished the year round. And I know that in many lakes the panfish got bigger after year-round fishing began.

I remember we had a discussion on the Solunar Tables which deal with feeding and activity periods of fish. I think it was Tony Lane who said, "I was out at Minnetonka the other day and I had along a copy of the *Minneapolis Tribune* with the Solunar Tables. I looked at it and decided not to go out on the lake until a major period started. I went out on the lake at the recommended time and in a half hour I got my limit of crappies!" With that fishing story he "proved" that the tables might work. I didn't know he had that experience, but it was timely for our discussion on the show.

Another time we were debating the question, "Does Noise Scare Fish?" So we hired Jack the Frogman, a well-known local diver to help with an experiment. We went out to a lake and Jack went down to the bottom, right below our boat. Somehow he signalled us when the fish had settled in around him. We started the outboard motor and, would you believe, instead of going away the fish all came up underneath the boat! They left for a few seconds and then they all came back to see what had spooked 'em—like a bunch of curious kids.

Catching Bass in Mid Air
Stu Mann Versus Leo Pachner

One of the most fun things I ever did fishing involved Leo Pachner, who in my estimation was one of the greatest bass fishermen in the United States. Leo was one of the founders of the Sport Fishing Institute. He was from Momence, Illinois and learned how to fish in the river there.

Anyway, Leo and I were fishing for largemouth bass on Cub Lake near Outing, Minnesota. That's a small lake with a lot of good pockets. We were in a boat, casting in toward shore, when I hung my line over a tree branch. The branch wasn't too high. Leo said, "Now wait a minute, Stu. Don't do anything." I always learned a lot from Leo, you know.

Then he said, "Jiggle it. Jiggle it some more." So there I was, jerking on my line, with the plug dancing up and down about four feet above the water. All of a sudden this bass leaps out of the water and hits my plug in mid air! I couldn't believe it!

Leo said, "You know, Stu, I have caught more bass in mid air than you can imagine—either like this with the lure hanging from a branch or before the lure hits the water on a cast. It's the biggest thrill I get bass fishing."

So the next year we had a contest to see who could catch the most bass in the air. Leo caught five that year and I caught three. I'll never forget one of those catches. It was on Lake Koronis at Paynesville, out of Marvin's Modern Cottages. I used to catch a lot of bass there, and I had one pocket in the weeds that was my favorite. It was on the side of the lake across from the highway.

The panel on Stu Mann's "Minnesota Outdoors" TV show: (left to right) "Uncle Ed" Franey, trout fishing expert; wildlife artist Roger Preuss; Cliff Sakry, conservation authority; host Stu Mann; and photographer/archery buff Tony Lane.

I had made about 15 casts into this pocket with a red and white lure made by Ernie Weber. Nothing. Then, on the 16th or 17th cast, I hooked a bass about two feet off the water. It weighed 5 pounds 14 ounces. And boy did it give me a battle!

I also got a nice one that way at Lake Geneva near Alexandria, on an opening weekend of the bass season. Jack Connor, the *Minneapolis Tribune* Outdoor writer, was in the boat with me. That bass weighed between 3 and 4 pounds. Jack couldn't believe it!

Rollie Johnson

WCCO, Corrie's, and a Fishing Contest

For 16 years I had an outdoor show called "Hunting and Fishing" on Twin Cities' Channel 4. I guess I got it started in 1951, not long after WCCO got its TV franchise. I did the show 12 months a year, some years, especially when Hamm's Beer sponsored it.

Hamm's had the bear going in those days, and it was very popular. When I did the show for just part of the year, we'd start right around the first of May, just before the opening of the fishing season. And we'd wind it up around the first week in October, after hunting got started.

We started the fishing contest right off the bat with our first show. The winners would appear on the show. It was a matter of getting the guy in there, holding his fish, telling us how he caught it, where he caught it, what kind of bait he used, and other interesting details. Maybe he'd name the friends who were with him on the trip. And then we handed him his prize. We gave those prizes out every week and we stuck 'em right in their hands! The season winners were really double winners—a weekly prize plus the big prize.

The fish were entered at Corrie's sporting goods store on Marquette Avenue in Minneapolis. WCCO really had the contest, but the fish were weighed and displayed at Corrie's. Corrie's was our only official weigh-in station. The fish had to be delivered, in person, to Corrie's.

We had one of those x-ray type machines, like the foot-scopes they used to have in shoe stores. Mothers would bring their kids in, and the kids put their feet in the thing, and you could look down from the top and see how the feet fit in the shoes. Well, we got a hold of one of those machines and we'd put the fish under there to discover if anybody did anything to alter the true weight of the fish.

We found two cases where they tampered with fish weights. One guy put lead down the gullet of a largemouth bass, some of that real soft lead that you can roll up like a tape-measure. Fortunately, he didn't put enough in, so he wasn't among the winners anyway. All we did with that guy was to write him a letter and tell him never to try it again.

But another guy would have been a first-place winner in the walleye division if we hadn't discovered his trick. In fact we got a copper down to the studio. We had it planned so that when he'd report to collect his prize on TV the cop would take him away and arrest him for falsification. We were gonna show that he had taken a tobacco sack, like a Bull Durham pouch with a draw-string, and filled it up with wet sand and BB shot from a shotgun shell. He had mixed the shot and the sand. That was good and soft, something you wouldn't feel. So he shoved it down the fish's throat. But it showed up really good on our examining machine.

182

Somehow word must have gotten to that guy, because he never did show up for his prize. We were gonna give it to him good in the studio!

Warmath, Corrie, VanKonynenburg, and Johnson
Shooting the Rapids with a "Touch of the Lord"

When I had my Hunting and Fishing show on WCCO-TV, I shot most of the film myself. For fishing films I'd make up a party of at least four fishermen. Usually one or two of these guys would be well-known, nationally known, if possible.

This one time, in 1965, I arranged a fishing trip for Murray Warmath. At that time he was head football coach at the University of Minnesota. Murray had taken two Gopher teams to the Rose Bowl, losing to Washington in 1961 and beating UCLA in 1962. He collected a national championship and a coach-of-the-year title in the process. Along with Murray were Mel Corrie, who for many years operated what I thought was the very best sporting goods store in Minnesota, and F. VanKonynenburg, the president of WCCO-TV and WCCO radio at that time.

Our destination was God's Lake in northernmost Manitoba, Canada, where Barney Lamm of Kenora, Ontario operated two outpost fishing camps. There was the God's Lake camp, mostly for lake trout. And there you could fish walleyes in a narrow but fast whitewater stream which flowed into God's River. And there was an outpost camp at Knoochin Rapids on Island Lake River for speckled trout.

Flights to these outpost camps all originated at Barney's main camp on Ball Lake. It was a big luxury layout with plenty of walleye and smallmouth bass fishing right there in front of your cabin.

After a pleasant four-hour flight to God's Lake we had time to get in plenty of super lake trout fishing, everybody getting the limit of 10 to 21-pounders. Warmath caught the largest one, 21 pounds 8 ounces.

We had a pleasant stay at the God's Lake outpost camp that night. And after a great breakfast we made ready for the float plane to pick us up for the trip up God's River to its confluence with Island Lake River. Once up there, and after a two-hour ride by outboard motor, we stopped at that small fast-water river to do some casting for walleyes. They bit so fast that all four of us frequently had fish on at the same time. The best fishing was just

below a 20-foot falls near an Indian graveyard. Neither of our
Indian guides would go within a hundred yards of there. Must
have been superstition or something. Anyway, we had to beach
them while we fished and handled our own canoes.

It doesn't take long for your hands and arms to get tired with
that kind of fishing. So it was off to a pleasant spot on the Island
Lake River for a great lunch of fresh fried walleye. Then, after a
short snooze, we went on to the outpost camp at Knoochin Rapids
where we spent the night eating, drinking, and telling lies.

The next morning we were scheduled for a trout fishing trip up
Island Lake River. We expected the world's greatest speckled trout
fishing with a fly rod. But we were in for quite a surprise. What
happened next made the whole trip most memorable for me, as
well as for my companions, I'm sure.

First we drew straws to see who fished with whom in the morning. We would change partners for the afternoon. We always
worked it this way. And, of course, certain wagers were an important part of the deal. Mel Corrie and VanKonynenburg were
paired, so they got into their 18-foot freighter canoe with 10-horse
outboard. Murray Warmath and I loaded up a second canoe. You

184

see, each canoe had two Indian guides, one up front and the other in the rear to run the outboard.

Now I had forgotten a very important item, the iced-down cooler with Lord Calvert and Coca-cola. So I had to run back to our cabin for that. Meanwhile, of course, Van and Corrie had taken off, and they were out of sight right away. At Knoochin Rapids, Island Lake River is narrow, deep, slow, and very twisty. There were so many sharp turns in the river. But we knew that Van and Corrie were ahead of us, somewhere.

Both Warmath and I tried to converse with our Indians and soon learned that they spoke no English, and understood very little. So when we asked "how much farther yet?" they'd answer with something like "8 o'clock"! And when we asked what time it was they'd answer "five miles"! The rest of our conversation was by hand signals.

After about an hour and a half on the river there was still no sign of the canoe ahead. The river was wide and fast now, and we began to hear a faint roar. Pretty soon the noise grew into the loud roar of a terrible rapids! We assumed that Mel Corrie, Van, and their guides portaged up and over. But our guides motored directly into this raging rapids!

I figured this was the end, so I started to focus my Bell & Howell for some footage that might serve as a clue for those who'd later discover us and our equipment. The Indians paid no attention to our pleas. They kept on going. I soon had to give up on any thought of pictures, because heavy spray from the falls covered my lenses and view finder.

Well, believe it or not, with the outboard wide open, and both Indians using their paddles to guide us around the huge boulders, we made it to the top. We could breathe again, but still no sign of Corrie and Van. The next 20 minutes or so were pleasant-going in smooth water, so we celebrated with a "touch of the Lord," as we called it.

Then more woes. We were heading into another falls, higher and longer than the first one. Good God! Were they going to motor up this one, too? Yes they were, and they did. About five minutes beyond this second falls we spotted our companion canoe, with Van, Corrie, and their two guides, firmly tied to a shoreline tree. They were also "celebrating." After all, they had the identical hair-raising trip we had!

We rigged up and started fishing for the famous speckled trout. We fished for a half hour, but not a speck of a trout! We got a jillion banana-sized walleyes instead. Then, about 11:30, the Indians decided they'd fillet some walleyes and make lunch.

Now get this! Right after lunch and a short nap the Indians indicated we had to start back already. You know, that "five miles" and "8 o'clock" stuff again. But they did get us to understand that it was a long trip back and that they had to go down those same rapids while it was still daylight.

So, hell! Here we go back with no trout! But we were thankful we still had our lives. I did film the trip back, down both rapids, with no spray on the lense this time. But with only the Indians' paddles to guide us through the raging water, things were bouncy. The film I got was just a swirling mass of white water. Useless.

We made it back to camp all right. But the next day two Indians and two fishermen didn't make it back okay! Their canoe got out of control and crashed into one of the big boulders midway through a rapids. One fisherman was killed, one Indian drowned, and the other two were found the next day, huddled on the bank of Island Lake River.

That night we were unhappy as hell waiting in our cabin, waiting for morning when our plane was due to pick us up about 10:30 for the trip back to Barney Lamm's main camp. Our trip for speckled trout had been a flop. But just a few hours before our scheduled departure I asked if there might be trout in the Island Lake River where our cabin was. "Why yes!" said the cook, "Lots of them!"

So Van and I got an Indian to take us out. On the way to our canoe I told Van I would never again fish with any guide who couldn't speak or understand English. Our guide was walking ahead of us and he heard me. He turned around, and in good English he told me, "Mr. Johnson, I don't blame you, but I'm glad you like to fly fish for trout because they are right here!"

And they were, right in front of our cabin! I caught a limit of 6 to 8 pounders in no time. Van did not fly fish so he just came along for the ride. But there were those trout, right in front of our cabin. And to think we had risked our necks on that ride through the rapids, way up the river, with no trout to show!

With our fish cleaned, iced, and loaded, we got on the plane. And we all had another "touch of the Lord" on our way back to Kenora!

Gerhardt Block, "Mr. Walleye"

Gerhardt Block's fantastic walleye catches earned him the title of Ortonville's "Mr. Walleye." More than anyone else, he helped make Big Stone Lake famous for big ones. Block had fished Big Stone all his life, but the lunker headlines began appearing after he and his wife set up The Block 'n' Tackle Shop in Ortonville in 1964.

Hellcats and Lunker Walleyes on
Big Stone Lake —
How It All Started

It was in the fall, around 1967. I was fishin' down by the outlet, where the Minnesota River leaves Big Stone Lake. It was daylight, in the morning. A guy by the name of Paul Steltz was down there casting. And he got snagged. He brought the snag in to shore, and on it was a big plug. He got lookin' on the plug's lip and it said "Hellcat."

I was fishin' with a Pflueger Shiner Lure in the "Strawberry Blonde" color. It was a plastic plug shaped somethin' like a Rebel or a Rapala. Around that time I had been catchin' a lot of fish on that lure.

Steltz put on the Hellcat that he found and fished with that. He didn't catch any, but I caught two big walleyes on my Pflueger Shiner Lure, the Strawberry Blonde. So he looked at my color and then went home to find some red and orange paint. He put the paint on the Hellcat and then he took a rag and wiped across it. You know, he came back down there and caught six of the biggest walleyes that you ever wanted to lay your eyes on! On that Hellcat that he painted like my Strawberry Blonde!

That was the only Hellcat we could find. So we fished that way for the rest of that fall, Steltz with the Hellcat and me with my Pflueger lure. Steltz caught way more fish than I did.

We looked all winter, through all the magazines and catalogs, and couldn't find out where Hellcats were made. Finally Paul found a book in somebody's basement that showed the Hellcat, made by Whopper-Stopper in Sherman, Texas. He wrote to them and ordered some. But they wrote back and wouldn't sell to him because he was just a private fisherman. They'd only sell to a bona fide dealer. I had the bait shop so he brought the letter in to me. They sent me some Hellcats, the 3/4 oz. size, sort of silvery on the sides and dark on top. I started painting them that strawberry blonde color and I'd sell 'em. I'd paint half the night!

Then one time the fish really started hittin' and the people started buyin' Hellcats faster than I could paint 'em! About that time I got a letter from Whopper-Stopper. They said, "We understand you're losin' a lot of sleep paintin' Hellcats at night. Send us a sample and we'll paint 'em for ya!" Then we had Hellcats with the right color, without all the paintin'!

Back then, hardly anybody knew about walleyes at my pet spot. At first I'd go down there, get my fish, and keep it quiet. But I was selling bait, and pretty soon the word got out all over. I'd go down there, make a cast or two, and get a lunker to show off.

One morning it was 20 minutes to seven. I said I was going down to get a fish. My wife said she just about had breakfast ready. I went down there and two guys were fishin' there with chubs. They had been fishin' since midnight. I threw out and I got one, a nine-pounder, right away. Those guys said, "It didn't take you long!"

But that's the way it was. One cast and I'd have one. I was selling bait, so I'd go to the radio station, or the newspaper, and tell 'em about the big fish. In spring and fall, especially in spring, the chubs would work good. So I'd sometimes sell 70 or 80 dollars worth of chubs in one night!

Of all the nights I put in with those Hellcats I have a few favorites. I'll tell you about one. There was about six of us that had been fishin' down there. They'd start in about 4 o'clock in the afternoon and fish until 8 or 9 in the evening. But the fish wouldn't come in until late. And by that time they were all wore out from castin' for five hours. So they made out that the next night they wouldn't come until 8 o'clock, or 9 o'clock, and fish later.

So that next afternoon the barometer started droppin'. And the wind turned and went into the south. I said to my wife, "I want to

get out of here by 5 o'clock tonight. The walleyes are gonna be in."

She said, "Aw, you and your walleyes!"

Well, I didn't get out at five. But I got down there about quarter to six. I threw out north, and that heavy south wind carried my Hellcat way out there. I had 6-lb. line on the reel, underneath, and I had added some 8-lb. test line. I felt the splice go through the reel and the rod guides when I cast, so I knew I was on the 6-lb. line by 10 feet or more.

My heart just about flipped when I got a lunker on right away. I took him real easy and brought him in a ways. And after I got that

6-lb. line inside the reel, and cranked a few times, I felt pretty good! I got that fish in and it was a 15-lb. 2-oz. walleye! That was the biggest walleye I've seen from Big Stone Lake.

Then I dropped everything. I netted the fish, got it out of the net, left the net lay, and I said, "Well, I'll never put this one on a stringer."

So I brought it up and put it in one of my aerated minnow tanks. Then I went back to the lake and found everything laying just the way I left it, and went back to fishing. I caught 19 more walleyes! But the little ones were in there so bad. If you got a fish after reeling three feet it was a small one, maybe 1-1/2 to 2-1/2 pounds. But if you could retrieve for five or six feet, and then get a hit, you'd have a bigger one!

I had those fish by quarter to eight. I threw most of 'em back, but I brought home six good walleyes. Now at quarter to eight these other boys all come down there. The preacher, Teske, Heine Lentz, and the others. Heine threw out his Doll Fly and he got an 11-pounder. Teske threw out to the right of me and I think he got a 4-1/2-pounder. And they fished all night then. A guy named Hodge, the head of the light department at Madison, was there too. They fished all night, and besides those two walleyes they had only two northerns when they were done!

That sure was something. The night before you couldn't get a bite before 8 or 9. On this night it was all early. And I was there!

Cussin' the Carp

We've foul-hooked walleyes while crankin' in Hellcats. And that is a battle! This Paul Steltz was bringin' in a fish one time, lettin' it go and jerkin', and he was cussin'. A carp, he thought. And I said, "Don't you want that walleye?"

He said, "Ha! Did you ever see a walleye run sideways like this? Three or four runs sideways?"

I said, "I'm seeing it now!"

And the reason he ran like that was he had it hooked in the top fin. He had a walleye snagged but didn't know it. But I saw his tail when he rolled once. Steltz thought it was a carp!

Gerhardt's Introduction to Pimple Fishing

I'd seen guys use Pimples, jig 'em just right, and they'd get fish. I'd go try it and get nuthin'! They was doin' something right and I

190

was doin' something wrong. It's gotta be done right. There's a right way of workin' that Pimple.

You can follow the directions that come with Pimples and Doo-Jiggers. Give 'em two or three jerks, pulling up fast, and then let 'er sit one minute. Well, I've had the best luck on the sit with both Pimples and Doo-Jiggers. The Doo-Jigger's made by the Pimple outfit. I've caught a lot of walleyes on the Doo-Jigger, more than I've caught on the Pimple. But I started with the Pimple, quite a few years ago.

The guy's name is Harry Ball. He was a road contractor from Fort Wayne, Indiana. He used to come up here to fish with his buddy, Roger Belgum, a mailman from here. I was in the bait business here, in the Block 'n' Tackle Shop.

Old Harry came in there and threw two 12-1/2-pound walleyes on the rug. He said, "There. That's what they look like! There's a pair of walleyes for ya!" He got 'em on the Swedish Pimple.

A little later I saw Harry standing in the pool hall. I walked in there and I said, "Are ya goin' fishin', Harry?"

"No!" he said. "I'm not goin' fishin'." But he had on his parka and his foul weather gear.

And I said, "Naw, it's too cold today. I wouldn't go either, Harry, if I was you. I'd stay in here where it's warm."

So after he went out I watched him, and followed him. Now I had a cabin on Big Stone Lake, at Meadow Brook on the Minnesota side. And Harry parked his truck near my cabin, on my property! He walked straight out onto the lake. I walked out too, but I stayed about two blocks away from him and watched.

He was workin' that Pimple up and down, and he got a good walleye! I saw him go way up high with that Pimple, really movin' it. Then I left. I didn't go over to him.

The next day I saw Harry in Sigloh's sporting goods store. He said to me, "Was that you following me?"

I said, "Yah, I believe it was." And we gave each other a bad time.

He said, "That's a lot of nerve!"

I said, "Harry, it ain't a bit more nerve than it took for you to trespass and park on my property." It was all sort of funny.

But he was the first guy I really saw usin' the Pimple. He was usin' a plain #4 or #5 Pimple, a small one, and he got nice fish. That's how I got started. I used the Pimple after that, but I never did as good on that as I did on the Doo-Jigger. They were part red and part chrome. Then there's blue and chrome. We used the big

Do-Jigger

The Do-Jigger, made by the Swedish Pimple folks, Bay de Noc Lure Co. of Gladstone, Michigan.

one. And man did we catch lunkers on that! Heine Lentz and I used to go fishin' together. He was a great fisherman. In the summertime he was a Doll Fly man. He'd use all sizes of Doll Flies, depending on what he was fishin' for. He'd get walleyes, northerns, and you name it.

Lunker Walleyes Through the Ice at Big Stone
Some Blockbuster Hits

It was on a Sunday, before Christmas. The ice wasn't too thick yet, maybe 10 or 12 inches. But I was driving out with my pick-up. I had a big fish house and a little house out there. The little house had been straight out from the Peninsula, but I moved it a half a mile south.

I got the house set up, put a minnow on, and went down with my Doo-Jigger. I went to pull up and I hooked the bottom. It wouldn't come. It was a lunker! I finally got him started but he rolled off. That same thing happened three or four times.

After that, in a little more than an hour, I caught 19 walleyes! I never did land a lunker, but when I came home I had six nice walleyes, seven and eight-pounders. And I had one 9-pounder. That ain't too small! But I had some bigger ones that got off. And I threw back a lot of three and four-pounders.

192

I looked at my watch when I started, and that was at 2:30 in the afternoon. At 4 o'clock they started to slow up. And I was gettin' tired of putting fish back in the hole. I couldn't get a lunker anyway. That was a good spot! I stayed there for a long time that winter and got some real beauties.

One winter I had 61 lunkers on and landed 20. Forty-one got away. I'd come home and tell my wife, "Another big one got away." She'd say, "That's the old story, isn't it?"

I had a lot of them right up to the ice. I know what my trouble was. It was too light a line. I couldn't hit 'em hard enough! I used 10 lb. test line. Then I went to 15, and finally to 17. One day it was stormin' and, boy, I got three out of four! I finally snapped that 17 lb. test line on the fourth one. I did bring in three dandy lunkers.

Heine Lentz, my buddy, would go to Hutchinson to visit his daughter. He'd stay about three or four days. And every time he went to Hutchinson I'd make an extra big hit on fish. I'd bury 'em outside here and show 'em to him when he'd get back, so he knew I got 'em.

But we got a lot of fish together, too!

"Bud" Denny, From Bena
on Big Winnie

The Denny family has long been associated with the fishing business at Lake Winnibigoshish. It started when Bud's dad, Guy Denny, brought his family from Owatonna to Bena in 1932. Fishing and guiding with small boats and outboards evolved into a larger fishing operation, Denny's Launch Service, begun in 1946. Over the years, the fleet grew from two launches to six big boats in the 1980's. Following are Big Winnie walleye stories from George "Bud" Denny.

Walleyes
A Cure for Sea Sickness?

The last week in July, about 1971, we fished a crew headed by Larry Johnson from 8th Crow Wing Lake by Nevis. I think there were 12 in the party and they came over for a day's fishin'.

It was really quite rough. The waves were probably six or seven feet high. We started out in the bay here first, out from Bena. Then we moved out further to the Middle Bar. And there we picked up about eight or nine walleyes. It was still quite rough there, waves maybe four to five feet high.

About this time we had eight or nine people sick. So I figured it was time to either go to the other side of the lake to fish in calm water, or to take 'em back in. I didn't want the day ruined for them so I moved to the other side of the lake. It took about three-quarters of an hour to get over there.

We got over there and fished. I moved a couple times, and the second move was a good one! We hit a place where the fish were bitin' pretty good. We were usin' spinners and nightcrawlers at the time, 'cause this was probably the last week in July.

Well, the fish had started to bite about 11:30 or so. Between then and 2 o'clock everybody recovered from being sick and they caught a limit of fish! Then we headed back. And the closer we got toward home the rougher it got again. What's funny is they enjoyed the trip back, rough as it was. They got sick on the way out and forgot about getting sick on the way home! The walleyes must have cured 'em!

Terrific Winnie Walleye Fishing

We were fishing with minnows, in August, around 1969, right out in front here in Bena Bay. My brother was along on that trip. We started right close in. There was only one other launch near us, the others being farther out.

We drifted down with a south wind and within a block after we started the drift we had 22 or 23 walleyes. We drifted on for another block and picked up about 10 more. So I went back to where we started and began another drift. Well, after just two drifts like that we had the limit of walleyes for everybody on the boat—14 people! And these fish ran from 2 to 7 pounds! That was terrific fishing. We were back at the dock at 20 minutes after 10.

You see, there was nobody in the bay, only one other launch down the line from us. Nobody had disturbed those fish. Nowadays, if you take a launch out here and start to fish a bar, somebody with field glasses will see you from five miles away and move in there. Then the next guy moves and the next guy moves and, the next thing you know, that launch has 8 or 10 boats around it. If fishing is halfways decent in the area you'll draw more launches and 15 or 20 more small boats, until you've got a fleet there in no time. This commotion makes the walleyes move from the top of the bar into deep water where they might not bite!

High Stakes

A few years back we fished a gang of farmers from near Breckenridge. They'd bet as high as a hundred dollars a fish! Now this was back in the 50's and 60's, when a hundred dollars was still a big bill!

The first fish in the morning was always a hundred dollars per fisherman. And some of them bet a hundred dollars a fish right straight through the trip, while others were betting five or 10 bucks a fish. Lots of times the engine box was just covered with greenbacks! Some of those fish got pretty expensive!

But they were always a good bunch to have along.

A Big One That Got Away

Every once in a while a walleye fisherman tangles with a big muskie. One time there was a fella here who had a Zebco. It was a new outfit that he maybe had used a couple times. We were trolling for walleyes down by Birch Point, about 2-1/2 miles east of our place. This was in the latter part of July and we had caught quite a few walleyes on that trip.

Well, he put on a big spinner, with a light sinker, and threw it out there. And something nailed it right away! Of course, this guy gave it a yank 'n' set the hook. And whatever it was—I don't know—it kept on going with his drag! So I turned the boat around and started to follow the fish. We were trolling and walleyes were actually being brought into the boat while we had this big one on.

I followed him up the line for maybe three-quarters of a mile, and then he turned around and started comin' back. So I turned the boat back, too. But the guy eventually ran out of line and the fish broke it off. We never saw what it was!

We've taken some pretty big muskies on our walleye trips. And we've taken a lot of 18 to 24-pound northerns on minnows and spinners. We've even caught some pretty nice northerns on leeches and nightcrawlers. But, boy, you've got to be pretty careful with the monofilament lines we've got nowadays. You can't horse around the way you could a few years back, when you had cable leaders, Prescott Spinners, and even June-Bugs. It's a different story now.

Dunkings Off Raven's Point

I've had as many as four or five guys in the lake at the same time—mostly in fun, though. There must have been 34 or 35 fellas at the place, all from the National Guard. I just had part of 'em on my boat, maybe 11 guys. We went over to Raven's Point, and they had a big party goin' on.

The fishin' was pretty good. We had probably between 45 and 50 walleyes, but they got feelin' pretty good in spirits and started throwin' each other in! About half an hour of that and I said, "That's about enough! I think we better head for shore before half of you drown." So we brought 'em in.

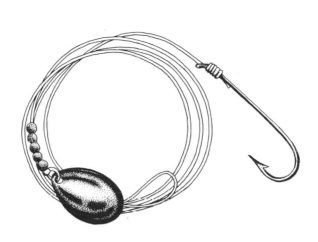

Little Joe "Red Devil" Spinner

First sold in the early 1960's by the Mille Lacs Manu-
facturing Co., Isle, Minnesota, then by Lindy/Little Joe
of Brainerd.

They had a good time. Of course they were soakin' wet. I think
there were two guys dry on the whole boat.

In a Storm Off High Banks

Storms? I've been caught in some good ones. On the wrong side
of the lake, too! I recall one in particular, in 1950. We had four
launches at that time, and I think I had eight people on my boat.
The wind was from the south/southeast at about 30-35 miles an
hour before we went out. And it was black!

For a while everybody debated about going out, but eventually
it was decided to go anyway. So we figured on starting a couple
miles south of High Banks, on the east side of the lake. That put us
only 3-1/2 or 4 miles from home, in case it didn't look good and
we'd want to go in. We stopped there and the fish weren't biting.
So we went on further, a couple miles more to High Banks, where

we ran into a bunch of walleyes. Everybody was catching fish to beat the devil.

This was just before the storm. We could see in the north/northwest that it was gettin' blacker than the dickens! Bob Tibbets, one of the other guides, hollered, "Aren't ya goin' in?" I said, "Yah, because it'll probably hit in a half an hour. If we can get in we'll be all right."

So he started in. But then the wind died down and he came back. The people wanted to fish some more because the fish were bitin' good. Well, they no more than got their lines back in the water and I decided to take off, because I had people in an 18-foot boat I was trailing behind the launch. So I took off and others went down the line. Some of them went up to High Banks Resort to dump people off. And other fishermen went into Tamarack Bay because they could tell. It was gonna blow pretty good!

But I didn't realize it was gonna blow a hundred miles an hour! Boy! I got down to the lower end of the Banks and there I sat by myself. And those waves were running 12 or 13 feet high, you know! And I had to take everybody out of the front part of the launch, out from under the roof, and set 'em back by the engine box so the boat would ride better.

She really howled. But the launch rode all right. And the only trouble with the trailer boat was they had to break the top off the minnow bucket so they could bail the water out. Everything stayed afloat. I held the boat into the wind, giving 'er just enough power to keep 'er steady. I wasn't too far from shore. I knew about where I was, and about how much water I had under me. If you keep things under control you'd be surprised at what you can do.

It rained like mad, and it lasted a good hour and ten or fifteen minutes. Then the wind shifted into the north/northeast. And when that happened I got the boat pumped out and started for home. That storm blew cabins off their foundations. It was a corker!

Jimmy Robinson, A Fisherman Too

Jimmy Robinson's fame as a trapshooter, waterfowler, conservationist, and outdoor writer stretches worldwide. His hunting and shooting tales fill thousands of pages. Jimmy's fishing exploits are less celebrated, but his devotion to angling was always there, dating back to boyhood days around the turn of the century. Here are some rare glimpses of Jimmy Robinson as fisherman and teller of fishing stories.

Governor Freeman and Old Tony

I used to own Spider Island in Mille Lacs Lake, near the south shore. This is quite a few years ago. And that was a helluva place for shooting bluebills.

I had a fella there, a caretaker by the name of Tony. He was a retired photographer from Minneapolis. I think he was about 80 years old at the time. Now I've fished for more than 70 years, but I've never seen a guy catch walleyes like that fella! I'm telling you, he was fantastic. He had a cane pole. And he'd go out there, around the island, and catch those fish. He'd catch five walleyes to my one!

Anyway, Governor Freeman, Orville Freeman, was just elected. And he was up at Mille Lacs on a fishing party, one of those annual affairs. I think they were having it at Hazelglade. Or at least some of them were staying at Hazelglade. So the Governor looks out at the lake and asks about the island. And they tell him, "That belongs to Jimmy Robinson."

The Governor says, "Well, I'll go over there because Jimmy's a friend of mine."

So he came over, with a couple of fellas, and they had dinner with us. Then he was gonna go fishin', so I told him, "Go out with Tony."

199

So he went out with Tony and he got a big fish on, a big walleye, and lost it! And old Tony started cussin' him. "Gol damn," he said. "You're the dumbest guy I ever seen in my life!" And Freeman was just elected governor, you know?

After they got back Tony came in and told me what happened. And I said, "Tony, that's the governor. You shouldn't have said that."

Jimmy Robinson (left) and longtime Minneapolis Star & Tribune *sports editor Charlie Johnson with Mille Lacs walleyes.*

He answered, "I don't give a damn who he is! The dumb son-of-a-bitch! He had that 7-pound walleye right up to the boat, and he blew it!"

That old Tony didn't care who he was!

Opening Day But No Fishing for Jimmy

Years ago I used to go up to Mille Lacs a lot, to Izatys, a well-known big resort on the south end of the lake. I'd go with Cedric Adams, the radio personality, and Charlie Johnson, sports editor of the *Star*. And there were others.

We went up there once when the opening was late. The lake was all froze in except right along the shore. And, oh God, it was cold. I'm telling you! I don't know how many years ago it was. Well, I'll tell you about when it was—exactly when it was. It was about the time Humphrey became mayor of Minneapolis, because I had a bet on him, 10 to 1!

Anyway, we went up there fishin'. It was Cedric Adams and his wife, Bill Hengen and his wife, Charlie Johnson and his wife, and Clara and I. It was really cold. And I never went out. I played gin rummy the whole time I was there. I didn't fish at all. That was probably the first time I opened a Minnesota fishing season playing cards!

Fishing Years Ago Around Perham

I was born in Breckenridge, Minnesota in 1898, but I moved to Canada in 1900. My father died that year. My mother moved Walter, my brother and me up to Canada with my grandfather, her father. He was a big farmer and he moved to Canada and went in the land business.

I stayed up there until 1905. Then I moved down to Perham in Minnesota, really Richville which is right next to Perham. Grandpa Robinson lived there. He was in the lumber business. Dower Lumber Company.

So we fished all those lakes around there. In the spring we used to go down to Marion Lake, about a mile from Richville. A creek goes out of there, and we used to spear—rock bass, largemouth bass, northerns, and walleyes. Right in that creek! We took 'em out by the bagload. I mean we really took 'em out by the bagload! There were no fishermen in those days. No resorts!

We used to fish Marion a lot. My grandpa put up a big slide

there for the kids, one that went right into the water. One time Walter and I went over to Marion, about the time a helluva big storm was comin' up. It was lightning and thundering.

There was an old shack there, kind of a summer cottage, but just an old shack. Walter got scared and climbed underneath there. But I was fishing on the point. And every cast out, with minnows, I got a nice rock bass! I caught 44 big rock bass, all rock bass and no other fish! With all the fish in that lake—all the pan-fish, big northerns, walleyes, bass—I caught nothing but rock bass all day!

And every time Clara and I drive around there I look over and say, "There's that point where I caught all those rock bass."

And then there was Dead Lake. That's where I killed my first duck, in 1905, at Cal Peterson's. We used to go out there walleye fishin'. It was cane poles and rowing. No outboards then. No reels. But lots of fish.

I can remember that Mr. Bixby lived on Dead Lake. He was a preacher who happened to have a big boat, like a launch. I think it was a sailing boat. My mother, Walter and I, and Grandpa and Grandma Robinson—maybe 8 or 10 of us—would go out there about once a week. We'd have our lunch along and just catch wall-eyes like nobody's business. They used to pickle the walleyes in those days, just like with suckers in the spring.

Jimmy Robinson's Eagle Lake Muskie

I got a great thrill from a muskie I tied into up at Eagle Lake. That's east of Kenora in Ontario. And it happened just a couple years ago. I never got the fish. But there was more publicity about it in the Winnipeg and Minneapolis papers than if a guy had really caught one!

You see, I was up there with Les Kouba. Les and his wife were in one boat. I was in another boat all alone with this Indian, a Chippewa. Clara didn't go out that morning.

I told this Indian, "You know, years ago, back around 1930, '31, '32, '33—all through the 1930's—this lake was one of the best mus-kie lakes on the North American continent. There was a world record caught here in 1939, right over there by McKenzie's Lodge."

And he says, "It's just as good now as it ever was."

"Now!" I says, "Don't tell me that!"

Before I go on, let me say that when we'd go up there to Eagle, we used to go in at Vermilion, take canoes, and then go way down

Spearing northerns "by the bagload," a common spring scene years ago. This action is at the Lake Osakis inlet, 1908. (Minnesota Historical Society)

about 30 miles south to get into muskies. And we used to get a lot of muskies.

He said, "It's just as good as ever, or better!"

I said again, "Now you can't tell me that! There's no muskies taken out of here anymore."

He says, "You know why? Nobody fishes muskies. They got no patience."

I says, "I'll agree with you there! Up at my duck camp in Canada a fella used to stay two weeks, then a week, then three days, and now two days. And you've got the same thing with fishermen. They all want to go home. They don't want to stay and fish. Hell, in the old days we used to fish for two weeks at a time!"

So I agreed with him on the patience thing. Then I asked him, "Where are those muskies?"

He said, "Right there!" and he pointed not far away, maybe between a quarter and a half a mile.

Well, I only had a small rod, a bass rod. But we went over there. He had an old tackle box. And as he opened it he said, "You know, I hadn't been muskie fishing for about five years. But this fella from Wisconsin came up and wanted to fish muskies. And I told him if you want to fish muskies I'll take you out for 'em. But you're not likely to get a bite or a follow for two or three days. He said, 'I don't care. I'm a muskie fisherman and I'll stay as long as I can.'"

And I guess the Wisconsin guy stayed for three days. Maybe he had a couple strikes, but he never got nuthin' for two days. And then on the third day he caught five muskies!

The Indian was telling me this. And he took this bait out of the tackle box and showed it to me. It was about a foot long, a wooden bait that was all bitten up. It was a good muskie bait, so he put it on for me. He said, "Anywhere over there."

I heaved it out. And bang! On the first cast I made a muskie hit that plug. The first cast! Unbelievable! I didn't get him though, so I brought the plug back in. And the third time, by God, I got him on.

Now I had this light line, see? And I was scared to death! I kept pullin' him and workin' him kind of easy. Then the damn muskie came in and was right there, next to the boat. The Indian said it weighed 35 to 40 pounds. Oh, it was a helluva muskie!

Then he started to get behind the boat, around the motor. So I said to the guide, "Here, you take the rod. I want to get that muskie!" He took the rod, which he worked with one hand while holding an oar with the other. And boy, he was an expert, that guy was. He worked with that fish, got it up there, and bang! He hit it over the head. The fish took a lunge, made a boil, and went right under the boat. But it was still on!

He worked and worked with that fish, maybe for 10 or 15 minutes. Then he got him up, that great big bugger, right along the lefthand side of the boat. It was right there. So he hit him over the head again. But this time the fish went down and broke the line!

That's a good story. Had we landed that muskie it would have been just another big fish caught. It wouldn't have meant anything. But it got off and it was a sensational thing for me, a big thrill.

Now this was about 11 o'clock in the morning. We were just about ready to go in. But I said, "Oh, the hell with going in now. I want to fish muskies!" Kouba had gone in because they were gonna take Clara and go into Dryden.

The Indian said, "We're gonna move." So we moved and I kept on fishin'. It was one of those days, a real muskie day. You only get them once in a while. We went all along there, for maybe three hours. I think I got 18 strikes—and never got one! Unbelievable! But I found out there still are muskies in Eagle Lake!

Gene Jenkins, Lake Vermilion Guide

Gene Jenkins' love affair with Lake Vermilion began in the 1930's when, as a young boy from southern Iowa, he made annual trips to Life of Riley Resort on Norwegian Bay. He learned area lakes and woods on outings with the local boys. Veteran fishermen like Everett Bystrom, Hank Eicholz, and father-in-law John Nylund helped make Gene a guide. As years went on, he pulled guiding trips from up and down the lake, but especially from the west end—in the neighborhood of Pehrson's Lodge, Little Sweden, Head-O-Lakes, Spring Bay, Red Loon Lodge, Vos's, and Wakemup Bay Resort.

A Stream of Bubbles Goin' Up the River

There was a fella by the name of Dave Stiles from Chicago. Dave was quite an amateur photographer who liked to take movies. He and his wife had been staying at Pehrson's Lodge most of the summer. As the summer wore on the fishing in Lake Vermilion turned lousy, so this couple and I planned a trip to the Vermilion River. They were ready to go home and wanted a batch of fish. They didn't care what they had, as long as they were fish!

We went up there early this one morning. Before going out we caught a bunch of little green leopard frogs. Now frogs aren't much good in Lake Vermilion itself, but they can be darn good in the river. Also, when many of the lakes have slow fishing in August, the river fishing can be super.

Anyway, we got out on the river and pulled in on this one reef. It must have been around 1 o'clock in the morning, a bright sunny morning. I told 'em I didn't know if we'd catch anything there at that time but that we'd try. So I anchored off on the opposite side of the river and got them set up. Neither one of them cared to cast, so I had them fishing in a back eddy off of this reef.

Now the first thing that came into the boat was a 15-pound

northern caught by Dave's wife. That fish made quite a commotion. We had wild rice, mud, lily pads, and everything else mixed in with it! Then they caught several small walleyes. All this time I hadn't put a line in the water, so I finally rigged up with a little rubber-core sinker, a small hook, and a frog. About the time I was ready to fish I happened to look up. And right on top of the reef, in maybe 18 inches of water, we saw something humpin'. It seemed like it never was gonna go down. All we saw was his coal black back roll over.

With that, I picked up my rod and threw my frog out there, about where I figured that big thing was headin'. In a couple seconds, no more, I had one of the damnedest strikes you ever saw in your life. I was using an Ambassador 5000 reel with 14-pound test line, and I never even slowed him down. There was just one big churn out there, and I mean to tell you that line sung off of that reel like it was gonna burn things up! When my line broke there was just one big stream of bubbles goin' up the river.

I was just dumbfounded. I couldn't believe I had missed a fish like that. Dave grabbed his camera and he got a moving picture of that string of bubbles goin' up the river.

Well, I quick rigged up again. About that time we saw a dimple, like a big crappie dimple on the surface. I flipped my frog out there and came up with a 6-pound smallmouth bass. That was a real trophy, and Dave recorded the whole catch on film. But I'm afraid my heart wasn't in it anymore. I had lost that other big one and it really bothered me.

Now this was just one trip when we tangled with big fish on the Vermilion River. There were others. One time I had a guy up there who was throwin' a 12-inch Rapala, one of those big ones. We went through a rock heap by an old railroad tressle. A lot of debris had floated in there and you had to pick your way through it all.

We popped around the back side of it and he threw this big Rapala out there. All we saw was this big V come through the water and suddenly something engulfed that Rapala. And that was the last we ever saw of it! The guy didn't clamp down on the reel. He was a better fisherman than that. I think the fish just took 'er all in one gulp and cut the line right away. My guess is that it was a big northern, because I've seen some awful big northerns come out of there.

Price's Stretch
People from Kansas City Go Down the Chute

One time, probably back in the 1960's, some people came up here from Kansas City to fish the Vermilion River. At the upper end there's a big rapids. I suppose the stretch is about a mile and a half long. There's a chute through there, and I mean it's fast water! The only time they'd shoot that was in high water times, and they'd do it with canoes. Nobody ever took a boat through there! It's called Price's Stretch.

I used to use that area as an ace in the hole because we could catch muskie, walleye, northern, bass, crappie, and bluegill. There was everything in there. When you couldn't catch fish anywhere else I'd take people up there and we'd get a mixed bag. Of course, you could only get into the shoal waters above or below rapids.

I had taken these two fellas from Kansas City up there and we had pretty good luck. Naturally, they wanted to go up there again but I was busy. So they asked if they could use my boat and I gave them the key. Now when I took people up there I'd pull into the old portage trail and walk on down below the rapids where we'd cast from shore a little bit. That's what these guys were gonna do. And

I warned 'em, "Don't go down near the chute with the boat! You know, if you ever pushed away from shore and didn't get that motor started, you'd be sucked right into that wild water. You might live through it and you might not!"

At the time we used an air-cooled West Bend motor on this little 14-foot boat. It wasn't real dependable in starting, especially if it was a hot day. But it was all right.

Well, they went back to fish there without me. I saw 'em the next day and they never said much about their fishin' trip. But before they left for home they called me up and asked me to come over to their cabin. So I went over to Pehrson's and they related their story.

It seems they had fished up above and hadn't had much luck, so they thought they'd go down and walk over to below the rapids, as I did. They didn't have any trouble pulling into the portage trail above the rapids. There they beached the boat and walked on down to fish. Then they came back to the boat. One of them climbed in and got the motor ready for starting. It was one of those where you had to wind the starter cord on the fly-wheel. About that time the other guy pushed the boat out from shore.

But the guy running the motor forgot to turn the gas valve open. He pulled it over and it wouldn't start. He said, "The next thing I knew we were starting down that chute!"

I said, "What did you do?"

He said, "Well, we both dropped right down into the bottom of the boat. And did we get a ride!"

That chute runs for maybe a couple hundred feet between sheer cliffs. And there's rocks stickin' out all over. These guys got through it, shot out on the other end, and hit a boat! Some fisherman was down there anchored, right below the rapids. They shot through there and ran right into him!

I asked 'em, "What did that guy say?"

I guess the guy looked up and asked, "Where the hell did you guys come from?"

They told him, "We came through there," pointing to the chute.

This fisherman replied, "Nobody comes through there!"

Well, they had to take the rest of the day to get a farmer and his tractor, plus a flatbed to haul the boat back up above the rapids to where I had it, under a bridge. So they spent most of their day just getting the boat back. That old cedar-stripped boat had some big scratches on it, but no holes poked. It weathered the ride amazingly well.

The Lindy Rig

A plain-hook/slip sinker live bait rig that stormed onto Minnesota's walleye fishing scene in the early 1970's. First marketed by Lindy's Tackle of Brainerd, then by Lindy/Little Joe.

That motor was only a horse and a half, or two. We just used it for trollin'. It was enough to get around there but you weren't gonna set any speed records with it. Besides, there's an awful lot of rocks in there. And there's lots of good smallmouth bass fishin' there, too. If you had anything bigger than that you'd have scared all the fish out of there.

The Trout Lake Portage and Across Vermilion at Midnight

In recent years the walleye fishing on Vermilion has come back strong. And smallmouth fishing is experiencing a boom, thanks in large part to tremendous publicity from Al Lindner and his *In Fisherman* magazine. I've always believed in Vermilion as one of Minnesota's top walleye lakes. But a number of years ago we had some lean times. In those years I was trying to build a reputation as a guide, and I owe much of my success back then to Trout Lake, just a half-mile portage off Vermilion.

In those tough years I'd take people from resorts on Wakemup

Bay at the west end of Vermilion on long trips into a number of other lakes in the area—lakes such as Oriniack (sometimes called Long Lake), Pine Lake, Trout Lake, and Little Trout. There are so many Trout lakes in Minnesota, so we call ours "Vermilion Trout." One summer I made 57 or 58 guiding trips in there. As for Little Trout, it didn't make much difference what time of the year you'd go there. You'd always catch a lot of walleyes there, even if they weren't the biggest. And you always had the chance of running into a big northern. We've taken northerns up to 25 and 26 pounds up there.

In my early guiding days I almost never went all the way from Wakemup Bay to the Trout Lake portage by boat. Instead, we'd drive south to Fraser Bay, about halfway down Vermilion, and then go by boat to the portage. Hell, the first years I guided for Mr. Pehrson the biggest motor we had was only a 10-horse. I remember when three of us went the whole distance to Trout Lake with that 10-horse on a 16-foot wooden boat. We got up into Trout, had our fishin', and got home all right, but it was quite late. Twenty-two miles by 10-horse on a loaded boat is a long trip!

Mr. Pehrson had a 25-horse Evinrude for his private motor. Eventually he put that on a boat for me, alongside a 3-horse troller. But it was a helluva trip even for a 25—an hour and 15 minutes! It took gas, too. We'd take four 6-gallon tanks, bait, rods, and tackle. Throw several people in with that gear and you were loaded!

So when I made that run into Trout Lake I knew it would be a long day. There was that traveling time, and I fished it hard. Old Hank Eicholz, one of the most well-known guides in the Cook area, used to say Trout Lake was "feast or famine." You got 'em or you didn't. Well, I was determined to get 'em, one way or the other. That's why many times it was quite late, dark already, before I got back. We'd run that 22 miles in the dark, with no lights!

A lot of times we'd be delayed on those Trout Lake trips because the old truck at the portage wasn't very dependable. One time when I figured on being back before dark I hit the Trout Lake side of the portage about 5:30, only to find that the truck was broken down. And there were 14 boats ahead of me!

I had two or three guys with me that day. And I was running an 18-foot Crestliner—one of those big deep jobs—with front navigational lights. If I remember right we had a 40-horse outboard on it, so there was no carrying that rig over land for a half mile. We had to wait for the truck repairs.

To get parts for that truck they had to go to Moccasin Point, about six miles on the Trout side, and then drive another 15 miles into Tower. Then it was back to Moccasin Point and a boat trip back to the Trout Lake Portage. They made the round trip and thought they had the part. But the part was wrong so they had to repeat the whole deal!

Finally they got the truck repaired and the line of boats started to move. Most of the boats in the line-up were from the Tower end of the lake and had to go only six or eight miles. Everybody knew we had the longest way to go, but nobody was about to relinquish their spot. It was after midnight when we got across the portage!

They had some lights rigged up at the portage, so I switched over to another gas tank and tied everything down in the boat. One of the fellas with me was a big heavy-set man from Chicago, John Schreiber. I remember him looking out at Vermilion when we got across the portage. You never saw anything so black in your life!

John looked out at the lake, then at me, and he asked, "Are we gonna go all the way home? Or just to Moccasin Point?"

I said, "All the way home!"

He said, "You'll never make it through all those narrows, around the islands, and over those reefs. You'll never make it."

With that I cranked up that motor and said, "You watch!" Man, I wheeled that boat around and opened 'er up. And I never slowed down for nuthin'! There was just enough starlight for me to see the tree contours, and that's all I needed.

When I'm out late my wife Marilyn never worries about me. She understands that I know my equipment and won't take a chance. I'm careful in rough water and electrical storms. I've never hesitated to lay up somewhere when the weather gets bad, and she knows that. If I'm not in during a storm she'll go over to the lodge and show the relatives or friends of my customers that she isn't worried. That helps them stay calm. But I'm sure that on some occasions over the years she's wondered if I really was all right!

Babe Winkelman

Call Babe Winkelman a "pro" fisherman. He conducts popular fishing clinics in Minnesota and surrounding states, fishes tournaments, promotes fishing equipment for big-name companies, writes about fishing, and spends many hours afield. Babe's introduction to fishing was a bit more humble than all that, growing up along Stony Brook between Foley and St. Cloud. Babe's stories involve central Minnesota largemouth and smallmouth bass—formidable foes, even for a pro!

Wading the Mississippi
When a Smallmouth Changed Course

I used to fish the Mississippi River near St. Cloud whenever I got the chance. It was close to home when I lived in and near St. Cloud. And the fishing could be fabulous.

You see, there's the NSP Dam on the south side of St. Cloud, and you've got the Sartell Dam up north. From the Sauk Rapids Bridge to the NSP Dam there's a whole section of river that few people bother about. There's some real deep water in the center of the thing, like 20 to 25 feet in some places. Get out of those depths and it's just full of sand and gravel shoals. You've got some big sprawling rapids in there, with plenty of big boulders and rocks. The smallmouths would sit right around those boulders. The best time of the year for fishing them was usually August and the first half of September.

My approach was to put on a pair of tennis shoes, and a pair of levis, jump in, and go fishing! Sometimes I'd be in water up to my waist while walking the deeper portions between rapids, but one could walk it all the way from St. Cloud to Sauk Rapids.

On this one day in the summer of 1974, I'm in the water, standing on the edge of a gravel shoal. I was throwing a little jig, just an old jig head with a crayfish on it. I'd thread a live crayfish onto that jig and toss it in around the rocks. I picked up two pretty nice smallmouth there.

Then I moved on toward this one big rock that always held a big fish every time I waded the river. I was expecting a big fish to be there, so I threw toward the rock. The jig 'n crayfish hit the rock and bounced down into the favorite spot. Nothing happened. But as soon as that bait got about three feet farther out than normal, boom! He hit! And he takes off upstream. Meanwhile I'm up to my waist in a pretty good current, but hanging on to that fish.

As I said, he's heading upstream, but suddenly the line goes slack! I thought to myself, "That son-of-a-buck is comin' right for me!"

So I'm standing there, reeling as fast as I can to gain back that slack. I wanted control of the fish. About that time I see this big smallmouth, and the line went right down between my legs! It was a huge fish!

He must have gone between my legs around 80 miles an hour! And there I am, standing on one foot trying to get my other foot up and over the line, and also trying to get the rod freed from between my legs. But the fish kept going and the line tightened up. Everything happened so fast! The line broke, the rod broke, and I lost my balance in the current. I did a backward somersault into the drink, and the bass took off. I never saw him again!

I've always figured that smallmouth was big enough to be a state record. I know I only saw a glimpse of him going downstream between my feet. But I've taken 6-pound smallmouth out of there and I know this one was considerably larger. At that time I guessed he was eight pounds. Of course, when you see a smallmouth that big, and that quick, imagination does all kinds of things, particularly to a fisherman who wants him to be that big! But he was huge!

Anyway, there I stood with everything messed up. The rod was a good Speed Stick. I don't know if I hit it on a rock, stepped on it, or what. Everything ganged up on me in a moment's time. I lost a bunch of tackle, and my crayfish got away.

A Bass Fisherman's Dream "Near St. Cloud"

The best largemouth bass fishing I ever had in my life, on any lake in any state anywhere, took place on a small lake near St. Cloud. I don't like broadcasting its name because it's a small lake.

It was the middle of October in that dry fall of 1976. I planned on working with a photographer that week, Gregg Anderson of Mankato. So I had to go fishing in order to find a good situation for taking fish pictures. It was to be a week of fishing and filming for my columns and articles, and I wanted to do it in the Brainerd area. But the DNR closed fishing in northern Minnesota because of the forest fire threat, so I told Gregg I'd try it around St. Cloud and let him know about my luck. I had guided in the St. Cloud area and I knew this lake pretty well.

The day was October 10. My brother Dave was supposed to go with me but he had to back out at the last minute. So I went down there myself. I had it in my mind that the bass should be really deep, and I fished deep most of the day. I hounded some sunken islands out in the middle of the lake where I fished quite a bit in the summer.

I was on this one spot in about 25 feet of water for about 20 minutes and I took a bass about 5 pounds. I was using a black Dingo jig with a big red-tail chub. This was a really nice fish so I worked that sunken island to death, and worked some more deep water to death, but I never got another bass out of there —just this one good one. I was backtrolling out there and working that jig, just like I was walleye fishing. But it didn't work.

So about 3:30, or sometime in later afternoon, I headed down toward the south end of the lake. I figured I'd try the shallows for awhile. There's a big reed bank down there with a slop garbage type bay in back of it. That's a prime spawning area for large-mouth bass in spring.

As I was approaching that reed bank I met two fellas in a boat comin' out. They recognized my boat so they pulled over to talk. They had been havin' the same kind of luck, with only two little bass. I asked 'em where they caught 'em. They said, "Right over here, in that reed bank. But forget it. We just beat it and beat it and there's nothin' much in there."

Well, I didn't have nothin' to lose so after they motored by I went over to that reed bank. Goin' down the front face of it the first time I hit one bass about three pounds and another one about two pounds. Then I thought, "if they're here on the front there might be bigger fish in back of the thing."

So I went around to the backside of the weed bank, and just as I rounded the corner I seen a big swirl right by the reeds. I dropped my spinnerbait in there and whoom, a 5-1/2-pound bass! I was using a big spinnerbait, one of Lindy's old heavy ones, modified by pinching a sinker onto the shaft to give me a solid 1/2-ounce head. I had a great big #6 Colorado blade on there that really rolled well when buzzing through the water. I always use big spinnerbaits like that in fall. Now they make 'em like that.

That 5-1/2-pounder was only the beginning! In back of this reed bank it got real shallow, maybe a foot of water. I'd throw that spinnerbait out, just start boiling it below the surface, and there'd be three or four big wakes coming toward it at the same time. It was just a question of which one would overtake the spinnerbait first. And they were all huge!

I was buzzing that spinnerbait with a steady retrieve, the blade working just below the surface. Nothing real fast. It's what they wanted because I'd get a tremendous strike on every cast. In a little more than an hour I took 42 bass, 18 of them over four pounds! I kept four fish that weighed over six pounds, up to 6-1/2-pounds, and I lost two that were just plain mind-boggling. All this time I was back in there by myself. About two hundred yards out from this reed bank were these other three boats—guys I talked to and two other boats. They were fishin' out there while I'm in back of this reed bank catching bass like I had never done before.

I'll never forget those wakes coming at my spinnerbait. Sometimes there'd be six big V's comin' from every angle. It happened on every cast, those big bass racing toward my bait. I've never seen fish, so many big fish, in that kind of a feeding mood. They were just plain nuts! When you're sittin' there throwing 5-pound bass back in the lake because you have a bigger limit, it's unbelievable. Maybe it was two hours, but no more than that, from the time I got into that reed bank until I went to shore. It was a bass fisherman's dream!

As I said, I lost two really big bass that afternoon. One spit the hook, and I guessed she went seven pounds or somewhere in there. Then I tangled with another giant, and that was quite a fight. I had 12-pound line on my reel and had caught all these fish. Then I hook this big sow and break my line. But there's about 30 feet of it trailing in back of the fish! She comes up out of the water, with my spinnerbait still in her mouth, and that line dragging back. She'd come out of the water and try to shake that spinnerbait loose.

Now it was only a foot deep in there, so I took after her with the trolling motor, chasing her through the weeds as fast as I could go, trying to grab that line! Three times she came up and broke water, shaking her head. Finally she threw the bait—when I was about five feet from catching the line. I know she was over eight pounds.

216

Babe Winkelman out fishin'.

'Cause I had those four fish over six pounds in the boat, and this fish seemed like it was twice as big!

I had one of those big Igloo coolers and an aerator system with me, so I kept these big bass alive in there. I took off from the lake and headed for Robbie Pollreis's place on Pelican Lake near Avon. It was dark already, so we took no pictures. We took the fish down to Rob's big live box in the lake. My plan was to keep 'em in there for a day or so until Gregg Andersen could come up.

As it turned out, Gregg couldn't make it the next day. It had to be the day after that. So that next morning Robbie and I went out on Pelican Lake after walleyes. The fishing was prime, just perfect. The second walleye I got was a 10-1/2-pounder! I also got an 8-pounder and a 7-pounder that day. In two days of fishing we had 11 walleyes over 6 pounds. Naturally, we put those big walleyes in

Rob's live box, along with the big bass. And that could have been our mistake.

Finally, here comes Gregg for the photos. We had those big fish in the live box, the weather was right, and everything looked great for pictures. One of those "perfect trips." Now I don't know if the big walleyes and the big bass got into a fight, or what, but they tore one end of that live box right out! The biggest bass, the 6-pounders, got out into Pelican Lake! Only two 5-pounders stayed in the box. The 10-pound walleye was gone. The 8-pound walleye was gone. All I had left was the 7-pound walleye and those two 5-pound bass.

So we got no pictures of those tremendous fish. But Robbie and his wife saw them. And I've got the memory. We did have some good walleye fishing on Pelican after Gregg got there—lots of good fish, but no 8 or 10-pounders.

A Minnesota Lunker List

An Honor Roll Of Lunker Minnesota Walleyes

18-1/2 lb.   Taken in the state fish trap on the Rat Root River at Rainy Lake in the spring of 1938. A memo in the Department of Natural Resources walleye file, dated July 14, 1950 states that a Harry Haran reported the fish, and that it weighed 18-1/2 lb. with eggs. According to the memo, the fish was sent down to the state Tourist Bureau and mounted.

17-1/2   First caught in 1918 in the state spawn-taking trap at Bemidji and reappeared in nearly every consecutive spawning run through 1929. Nicknamed "Old Silver Spot," this hefty female was also called the "Mother of Millions." According to Hjalmar Swenson, longtime Minnesota fisheries chief, Old Silver Spot came into the Mississippi River trap from Wolf Lake. She skipped a couple years and then showed up again.

17-1/2 lb.   A Minnesota angling record from the Sea Gull River caught by LeRoy Chiovitte of Hermantown on May 13, 1979. The fish hit a plain hook-minnow rig on Sunday morning of opening weekend. Chiovitte and his companions were fishing about a mile from where the river enters the southeast corner of Lake Saganaga.

16 lb. 11 oz.   Frequently listed as a Minnesota record from 1956 to 1979. Caught by Merle Pulliam, then of Davenport, Iowa, on May 12, 1956 in East Twin Lake near

219

Ely. Pulliam's name is consistently spelled wrong in the old record lists. And the fish is often credited to Basswood Lake, another mistake. Early press reports appeared in "Ely Fish Facts" published by the *Ely Miner* on May 19 and June 2, 1956.

A Leech Lake catch, 1896. Nice walleyes, but no 16-pounders! (Minnesota Historical Society)

16-1/2 lb.	Landed by John Norkoli of Finlayson, Minnesota at Sturgeon Lake in Pine County around September 1, 1949. Norkoli's fish was listed in the *Minneapolis Sunday Tribune's* "Fisherman's Scoreboard," 1949, and was often regarded as a Minnesota angling record for the next seven years.
16-1/2 lb.	Taken through the ice of Lake of the Woods by Mitch Rebarchek of Graceton, Minnesota on February 15, 1959, this fish won the WCCO radio ice fishing contest. In fact, the February 22, 1959 *Minneapolis Sunday Tribune* billed this fish as a new state record. However, the catch was made near Burton Island, in Canadian waters. Rebarchek's catch was part of a fantastic run of lunker walleyes at Lake of the Woods during January-February, 1959.
16-1/2 lb.	Reportedly caught by "a guide" while holding the fishing rod of Mrs. R. E. Ash of Hinsdale, Illinois on Whitefish Lake, probably the one near Pequot Lakes. It was never recognized as a record or prize winner, but it was mentioned in "Fisherman's Scoreboard" in the *Minneapolis Sunday Tribune*, August 21, 1949.
16 lb. 4 oz.	Another lunker for 1949! This walleye was caught about May 19, 1949, by Martin Hammersmith of Elmhurst, Illinois on Moose Lake nearly Ely. He was vacationing at Hibbard's Lodge. This fish looks really big in a picture published in "Ely Fish Facts" on June 11, 1949. It topped the list of big Ely area walleyes published annually in "Facts" until Merle Pulliam's 16-lb. 11-oz. fish took the lead in 1956.
16 lb. 6 oz., 16 lb. 4 oz.	These fish were reported by Curly Lehn of Bemidji as being caught by himself from Lake Bemidji around 1960. The fish received press coverage. They were mounted and placed in birch display cases for Lehn's trips to sport shows and fishing seminars.

16 lb. 2 oz.	This trophy was in the company of other lunker walleyes when it was caught through the ice of Lake of the Woods on February 16, 1959. It was the day after Mitch Rebarchek's 16 lb. 8 oz. catch, in the same area near Burton Island in Canadian waters. This walleye was one of five lunkers landed by Lars Olson of Williams, Minnesota that day, their total weight being a whopping 73 lb. 3 oz. on a scale at U.S. Customs headquarters in Baudette.
15 lb. 13 oz.	Caught by Richard Aldrich of Babbitt, Minnesota from Bear Island Lake near Babbitt on August 15, 1960. At the time of this writing, Mr. Aldrich's fish was the largest Minnesota-caught walleye to win a grand prize in the *St. Paul Dispatch-Pioneer Press* contest.

A Roster Of Giant Minnesota Muskies

54 lb.	Caught by Indian guide Art Lyons out of High Banks Resort, Lake Winnigoshish, on Wednesday, August 28, 1957. According to the *Minneapolis Tribune,* Lyons' muskie was 56 inches long. This fish was first recognized as Minnesota's record in 1976. The previous record, caught in Sabaskong Bay of Lake of the Woods in 1931, was disqualified for having come from Canadian waters.
52 lb.	Reported by the *Baudette Region* as being taken from Lake of the Woods in 1930.
52 lb.	From Cass Lake, reported by guide Cliff Riggles as his personal catch in the early 1950's.
51 lb. 1 oz.	From Leech Lake, May 19, 1973, claimed by Mike Kelner. From Anoka at that time, Kelner went to Walker to work on a boat. Kelner's story has his bobber going down while walleye fishing during on-the-water repairs. Kelner's fish had local skeptics shaking their heads. A would-be Leech Lake record muskie taken by a non-fisherman who didn't plan to wet a line, on a small minnow in-

Mille Lacs walleyes around 1920. Lots of 2- to 4-pounders, but no lunkers. (Minnesota Historical Society)

stead of the usual big tackle fare. This fish measured 59 inches long and 26 inches in girth. A photo of Kelner and this fish is often used in Leech Lake promotional literature.

50 lb. Caught by Stanley Kroll of Chicago on Wednesday, August 22, 1951, while fishing on Little Winnie. Kroll and his fish were pictured in the *Minneapolis Sunday Tribune* of August 26, and in the *Grand Rapids Herald-Review* of August 23, 1951. The Grand Rapids paper reported that Kroll's fish was "believed to be the largest fish of record ever caught here." The fish was entered in Earl Fuller's Booster Contest at Grand Rapids. That same week, guide Ted Fairbanks hooked a 40-pounder, and Joe Terpstra of Hollandale, Minnesota landed a 45 lb. muskie, both at Big Winnie.

50 lb. A "Big Mistake!" The *Minneapolis Tribune* of February 19, 1961, pictured state fisheries supervisor Hjalmar Swenson and chief game warden Francis Johnson with a trophy muskie and the following caption: "One of the largest game fish ever to come from Minnesota waters is this 50-pound muskie

223

which was speared by mistake at Lake Audrusia recently. The spearer turned himself in and was fined $25 in Bemidji municipal court. The fish, which measured 53-1/2 inches long and was 24 years old by scale examination, was confiscated."

48 lb. 8 oz.	Appears in old record lists, but with angler "unknown." The fish was reportedly caught from Deer Lake, Itasca County, in 1950.
48 lb.	Caught by C.J. Van Lith of Delano, Minnesota in Leech Lake near Federal Dam. Van Lith won the 1967 grand prize in the muskie division of the *St. Paul Dispatch-Pioneer Press* contest.
64-1/2 lb. ?	Found dead on Lake Pokegama near Grand Rapids by bait dealers in 1937. It measured 56 inches long.
62-1/2 in.	What might easily have been a Minnesota record muskie washed up on a beach near North Star Resort on Portage Bay of Leech Lake in October, 1978. It was found by resort owner Randy Anderson. The fish was 62-1/2 inches long, longer than any of the above-mentioned lunkers! It measured 5-1/2 inches between the eyes. One of the teeth left in its mouth was 7/8 of an inch long. (DNR News Release, November 21, 1978 and *Outdoor Outlines*, December 28, 1978)

Great Northern Pike

45 lb. 12 oz.	Recognized as a Minnesota record. The angler was J. V. Schanken, whose fish was a *Field & Stream* contest winner. The catch date was May 16, 1929.
44 lb.	44 lb.? Minnesota DNR files and the *Ely Miner's* "Fish Facts Scoreboard" list this 1947 catch by Joseph Stutz of St. Paul. The fish was reported caught in American Agnes Lake and was probably entered in the *Field & Stream* contest. The original *Ely Miner* report and successive "Fish Facts Scoreboard" rosters through 1956 call it a 40-pounder.

Suddenly, in 1957, probably because of a typographical error, the fish became listed as a 44-pounder.

41 lb.
Brought in by T. E. Nichols of Deerfield, Illinois in 1948 at Loon Lake in Cook County. This fish was listed in the 1948 "Fisherman's Scoreboard" of the *Minneapolis Sunday Tribune*. Some old state record lists ranked this as Minnesota's biggest northern pike.

40 lb.
Caught by Harry Glorvick of Minneapolis in 1956, according to the *Ely Miner's* "Fish Facts Scoreboard."

32 lb. 6 oz.
Listed as being caught by Ralph Stroot of South Dakota in 1949 by the *Ely Miner's* "Fish Facts Scoreboard."

32 lb. 4 oz.
Taken by Ted Diesslin of St. Paul in Bass Lake near International Falls, Minnesota. A *St. Paul Dispatch-Pioneer Press* contest topper in 1963.

31 lb. 13 oz.
Caught on May 14, 1977 by Ellard L. Skuza of Sauk Rapids, Minnesota. Skuza was fishing for walleyes on opening weekend at Mille Lacs Lake. His fish won a grand prize in the *St. Paul Dispatch-Pioneer Press* contest.

Some King-Size Minnesota Crappies

5 lb.
A Minnesota angling record taken from the Vermillion River, Dakota County, in or about 1940. The fish was caught by Tom Christensen of Red Wing.

5 lb.
This crappie may have exceeded five pounds, according to the late John B. Moyle, Minnesota fisheries biologist. A 21-incher, it was caught by a rough fish seining crew at Linwood Lake near St. Paul in winter, 1949. A life-size drawing of this "catch" sprawled across an entire page of newsprint in the *St. Paul Dispatch*.

4 lb. 4 oz.,
4 lb. 2 oz.

Old record lists and DNR files mention these two lunker crappies reported by Authur Coe of St. Paul, probably in the 1940's. The fish are credited to Tanners Lake, Ramsey County.

Alvin Bell of Minneapolis with a 3-lb. 12-oz. crappie he caught in 1965 at Southern Lake near Buffalo. The fish was weighed at Golden Valley Sports Center. (Minneapolis Star & Tribune *Photo)*

4 lb.	Reported by Willis Krueger, Wabasha, to fish researcher Raymond E. Johnson in 1949. The fish was caught some years before that in a commercial gillnet in the Mississippi River. It was weighed four hours after being found dead in the net. The fish, 8-1/2 years old according to scale sample analysis, measured 19 inches long. Krueger had it mounted.
4 lb.	Or 3 lb. 12 oz.? This fish was caught in Southern Lake near Buffalo, Minnesota by Alvin Bell of Minneapolis around June 20, 1965. Bell's biggest lament: The fish, which weighed 4 pounds when caught, had lost a quarter pound when weighed later. He was angling for sunfish when the crappie hit. Bell and his fish were pictured in the June 28, 1965 *Minneapolis Star*.
3 lb. 12 oz.	Caught in the Rainy River near International Falls in 1965. David Herrly of International Falls, the lucky angler, won the year's top prize in the crappie division of the *St. Paul Dispatch-Pioneer Press* fishing contest.
3 lb. 10 oz.	Taken from Rush Lake near Rush City, Minnesota on June 25, 1976, by Levi Enos of St. Paul. A *Dispatch-Pioneer Press* contest topper that year.
3 lb. 9 oz.	Pulled from the waters of Whaletail Lake near St. Bonifacius, Minnesota. Dorothy Ryholm of Richfield, Minnesota, fooled this one on May 23, 1978 and won the season's top crappie prize in the annual *Dispatch-Pioneer Press* contest.

Big Bluegills

2 lb. 13 oz.	A Minnesota record since 1948, from Alice Lake in Hubbard County. The angler was Bob Parker of Bemidji.
2 lb. 11-1/4 oz.	The largest bluegill entered in the *St. Paul Dispatch-Pioneer Press* contest from its start in 1953

through 1981. Ellard Skuza caught the fish in 8 to 10 feet of water on the edge of weeds at Mission Lake near Merrifield, Minnesota in 1970.

2 lb. 10 oz.   Caught by Dick Birger of St. Paul at Norway Lake, Ottertail County, on September 15, 1950. (DNR files)

2 lb. 9 oz.   From Silver Lake near Battle Lake, Minnesota. The angler, R. E. Somerfield of Nopeming, Minnesota, won the 1961 Grand Prize in the sunfish division of the *St. Paul Dispatch-Pioneer Press* contest.

2 lb. 8 oz.   Caught in 1949 at Lake Edward, Crow Wing County, by Elmer Moss of Minneapolis. His fish made the *Minneapolis Sunday Tribune's* "Fisherman's Scoreboard."

The following anglers entered Minnesota-caught 2 lb. 8 oz. sunfish in the *St. Paul Dispatch-Pioneer Press* contest:

Clint S. Hardy, Sr., Overland Park, Kansas on August 5, 1959, from Ten Mile Lake near Fergus Falls, Minnesota.

Francis Witte, St. Paul, from Lake Sally near Detroit Lakes, late summer of 1965.

Orville Helland, Duluth, Minnesota, from Fish Lake near Duluth in early summer, 1967.

Lunker Minnesota Largemouth Bass

10 lb. 2 oz.   State angling record, 1961-1982. This catch was reported by professional angler and Bemidji guide, Harold "Curly" Lehn, who claimed to have caught the fish in Prairie Lake, Itasca County, on June 28, 1961. Except for its late summer entry as frozen fish in the Corries-WCCO contest, there is no record of a Minnesota weigh-in, press coverage, or contact with Conservation Department officials in the weeks following this catch.

9 lb. 14 oz.   Caught in Little Horseshoe Lake on July 19, 1937

by L.C. Blomberg. Information is scant on this fish, but DNR records indicate it was a *Field & Stream* contest winner.

9 lb. 14 oz.   From Snail Lake, Ramsey County, 1948. This fish is credited to H. W. Kirchner of St. Paul. DNR files contain no specifics on this catch.

9 lb. 6-1/2 oz.   The biggest Minnesota largemouth bass ever to be entered in the *St. Paul Dispatch-Pioneer Press* contest, and a would-be Minnesota ladies' record. The fish was reportedly caught in Cedar Lake, near Whipholt, Minnesota, and entered in the St. Paul contest late in the season of 1961. That year, Rice won the contest, just as she had in 1960, and also placed fifth with an 8-pound entry. Interestingly, Harold "Curly" Lehn, who claimed the record largemouth in 1961, won the St. Paul contest in 1959. He and Ms. Rice would appear to be the all-time Minnesota big bass champions. No detailed stories of these catches appeared in the press, and Ms. Rice declined to discuss the big bass with the author. She did volunteer that she had a "guide": Curly Lehn!

9 lb. 4 oz.   Caught by 14-year-old Fritz Allen Schneider in Lake Washington near Madison Lake, Minnesota. Fritz's fish topped the Bass division of the *St. Paul Dispatch-Pioneer Press* contest in 1978, and was declared a state record in February, 1983.

9 lb. 3 oz.   Reported to have been caught from Lake Minnetonka in August of 1961 by Fred Cropsey of St. Paul. His photo and story appeared in the *St. Paul Dispatch* of Tuesday, August 8, 1961. This lunker failed to win a major contest because of the huge entries of Curly Lehn and Elaine Rice. Cropsey said he caught the fish in about 20 feet of water on a deep-running lure.

9 lb. 3 oz.   From Eagle Lake north of Willmar. The fish was claimed by Glenn Jansma of Willmar. It took third

place in the 1961 *Minnesota Outdoors-Willmar Tribune* statewide bass fishing contest conducted by Stu and Dee Mann, behind the entries of Curly Lehn and Elaine Rice.

9 lb. 3 oz. The 1967 season bass winner in the *St. Paul Dispatch-Pioneer Press* contest. It was entered by Donald Witte of St. Paul. Witte's fish came from North Long Lake near Nisswa.

8 lb. 15 oz. Often listed as a Minnesota state record between 1944 and 1961. The fish was reported caught on September 26, 1944 by Frank Adams of St. Paul in Rush Lake, east of the village of Sturgeon Lake in Pine County. Sturgeon Lake notary public Glenn E. Olson measured and weighed the fish, and witnessed Adams' statement. The fish was again measured by fisheries biologist Thaddeus Surber and John Salvator: 24" length, 19-1/4" girth, and 9-3/4" depth. According to Adams, the fish hit a "mouse plug" in shallow water.

Big Minnesota Smallmouth

8 lb. A Minnesota record since 1948, taken by John A. Creighton of Minneapolis from West Battle Lake in Ottertail County. The fish topped the 1948 smallmouth division in the *Minneapolis Sunday Tribune's* "Fisherman's Scoreboard."

7 lb. 6-1/2 oz. Caught by Ben Jackson of Virginia, Minnesota in 1962. A perennial all-time leader among smallmouth entries in the *Ely Miner's* "Fish Facts Scoreboard."

7 lb. 2 oz. Taken on a leech while fishing in six feet of water off the south shore of Mille Lacs Lake on October 2, 1977. The fish was caught by Don Jergens and weighed at Bitzan's Tackle Castle at the south end of Mille Lacs. Jergens had a 4-lb. 12-oz. smallmouth the same day. The fish was mounted.

Jon Sanger of Grand Marais with state record 23-lb. 6-3/4-oz. chinook salmon he caught in Lake Superior near Hovland on July 27, 1981. Minnesota's chinook salmon program began in 1974 when fingerlings were planted in the French, Baptism and Cascade Rivers along Lake Superior's north shore.

7 lb.	Caught in 1953 by Delores Skaden of Blue Earth, Minnesota and listed in Ely's "Fish Facts Scoreboard."
7 lb.	Listed in Ely's "Fish Facts Scoreboard" as being caught in 1948 by Donald Legge of Oak Park, Illinois.

Some Trophy Lake Trout From Minnesota Waters

43 lb. 8 oz.	A Minnesota record, taken from Lake Superior by Gustav Herman Nelson of Duluth while trolling near Hovland on Memorial Day Weekend, 1955. The fish weighed 47-1/2 pounds on a commercial fisherman's scale at Hovland; 43-1/2 pounds at Midway Service station in Grand Marais; and under 38 pounds at a contest weigh-in at Corrie's in Minneapolis the day after the catch. *Field and Stream* accepted the 43-1/2-pound weight. The fish measured 43-1/2 inches long, 29-1/2 inches in girth.
42 lb.	Caught by Harold T. Grover of Huntley, Minnesota in 1949. Grover was fishing in Lake Superior near Hovland. His fish was listed as a Minnesota record for six years.
33 lb. 14 oz.	Another lunker from Lake Superior near Hovland, caught by Lewis T. Bostwich of St. Paul in May, 1955. The catch was reported in the June 1, 1955 *Minneapolis Tribune*.

(From the 1940's to the mid-1950's, sport fishing for lake trout in Lake Superior yielded trophies between 30 and 40 pounds. A popular North Shore weigh-in station for lunkers caught in the prolific waters near Hovland was the Midway Service Station at Grand Marais. Following are some of the huge lake trout weighed in at Midway during the bonanza years. There were others!)

40 lb.	Howard Wood, Chicago, 1953
37 lb. 8 oz.	Oscar Anderson of Minneapolis, early 1950's
35 lb. 8 oz.	G.A. Lindquist of Cleveland, Ohio, 1954

35 lb.	H.E. Swanson of Minneapolis, 1949
33 lb. 12 oz.	Donald Wanstrom, Gibbon, Minnesota, 1954
33-1/2 lb.	Pearl Patterson of Newton, Iowa, around 1950
33 lb. 6 oz.	Steve Korperski of Wausau, Wisconsin, 1951
33 lb.	James Murdock, early 1950's
32 lb. 2 oz.	T.G. Dugan, St. Cloud, 1952
30 lb. 4 oz.	Herb Schuman of Long Lake, Minnesota, 1954
30 lb.	Orrin Gilbertson of Beldenville, Wisconsin, 1952

Through 1981, the largest lake trout catches ever listed in Ely's "Fish Facts Socreboard" were made by Eric Theden of Rockford, Illinois (34 lb. 8 oz., 1951) and Tony Janek of New York, N.Y. (44 lb., 1947). The author's research shows that Janek's 44-pounder came from Quetico Lake in Canada.

Brown Trout Beauties

16 lb. 8 oz.	A Minnesota record caught by Carl Lovgren of St. Paul from Grindstone Lake, Pine County, on Memorial Day Weekend of 1961. According to a newspaper report in DNR files, Lovgren's fish was 31-1/2 inches long, 21 inches in girth.
14 lb. 15 oz.	Caught through the ice of Straight Lake near Park Rapids by Janice Tigue of Osage, Minnesota in January, around 1972. The fish was taken in the evening on a minnow. This 32 incher was mounted by the late Henry Haug of Bagley and is on display at Fuller's Tackle in Park Rapids, where it was weighed. This winter catch was legal because regulations that year omitted certain language regarding "designated trout lakes."
14 lb. 4 oz.	Taken by C.E. Titcomb from the Arrowhead River on July 14, 1956. A *Field & Stream* contest winner. (DNR files)
14 lb. 2 oz.	Often billed as the largest German brown trout to come from the Whitewater River. Landed in

14-lb. 1-oz. state record burbot (eelpout), 35 inches long, caught by Leonard Lundeen of Duluth on February 3, 1980. He was walleye fishing through the ice of Deer Lake in Itasca County. The burbot is a freshwater member of the codfish family, occurring in most large lakes and streams of Minnesota from Mille Lacs northward.

	Winona County by Bill Venzol of Altura, Minnesota in 1948.
13 lb. 14 oz.	From the Whitewater River, below the old bridge at the Crystal Springs fish rearing station. Caught on a nightcrawler by Ed Krieger of Elba, Minnesota in late July, 1974.

Record Rainbow Trout

17 lb. 6 oz.	A Minnesota record, caught on Saturday morning, January 19, 1974 in Knife River near Lake Superior. Ottway "Red" Stuberud of Knife River, Minnesota caught the fish. This lunker was 36-7/8 inches long. Area fisheries manager Herb Johnson identified the fish as a "very typical rainbow" and observed three old lamprey marks on its skin.

| 15 lb. 7 oz. | Caught in Lake Superior by Cliff Lovold of Two Harbors on September 11, 1970. (DNR files) |

14 lb. 9 oz.   Another Knife River trophy, caught by Joanne Stover of Duluth on June 26, 1960.

14 lb. 8 oz.   Taken from the Arrowhead River by E.O. Culbertson on August 1, 1933. A *Field & Stream* contest winner (DNR files)

13 lb. 2 oz.   Caught by John Wilnamski of Duluth in Split Rock River, Lake County, in 1948. Listed as a Minnesota record in *The Conservation Volunteer*, July-August, 1950.

Big Brook Trout

6 lb. 2 oz.   Caught by Wesley "Bud" Smith of Grand Marais from Pine Mountain Lake in Cook County, May 20, 1967. This fish became a Minnesota record in 1979 with the ouster of a 9 lb. 1958 "record" catch from the Ash River which may never have existed. The new record weighed 6 lb. 2 oz. at Midway Service in Grand Marais. Smith received a citation from *Sports Afield* magazine. Never suspecting his fish would be a record, Smith's family ate the big brookie. The fish hit a medium-sized red-white Dardevle with copper backside.

6 lb. 1 oz.   From Pine Mountain Lake, Cook County, June, 1977. This near record hit a nightcrawler behind flashing cowbells trolled by Yvonne Sabyan of Duluth, who was fishing with her husband, Tom. The fish was weighed at Midway Service in Grand Marais. It was 27 inches long.

5 lb. 7 oz.   The most short-lived brook trout record in Minnesota history! With the ouster of a long-standing record in spring of 1979, DNR officials gave this trophy the new title. It was caught by Byron Lynn in 1946 from the Isabella River. DNR had few details, although the fish was registered with *Field*

& *Stream* magazine. Wes Smith and Yvonne Sabyan soon came forward with their 6-lb.-plus trophies.

Mud Cat Whoppers

70 lb.   A St. Croix River lunker caught by John Lee Roberts of Garden Grove, Iowa near Marine on St. Croix in 1970. A Minnesota hook 'n' line record.

68 lb.   Taken from the St. Croix River by Ralph Ligget of Des Moines, Iowa, who was in the same fishing party with John L. Roberts who caught the above-mentioned 70-pounder. The operator of the Marine Boat & Canoe Service told the *St. Paul Pioneer Press* that the Iowans' fish were more the result of skill than luck, that they had been making good catches for years.

60 lb.   Caught by Al Stoll of Stillwater in September, 1960 while fishing for sturgeon on the St. Croix River about three miles above Stillwater. The fish measured 52 inches long and 31-1/4 inches in girth.

Updating the Minnesota Lunker List

We invite you to let us know of additional whoppers that should be in future editions of this lunker list. Use these guidelines:

Walleyes—over 15-1/2 pounds

Saugers—over 5 pounds

Muskies—over 48 pounds

Northerns—over 30 pounds

Largemouth Bass—over 8-1/2 pounds

Smallmouth Bass—over 7 pounds

Crappies—over 3-1/2 pounds

236

BEHOLD THE FISHERMAN
HE RISETH UP EARLY IN THE MORNING AND DISTURBETH THE WHOLE HOUSEHOLD. MIGHTY ARE HIS PREPARATIONS. HE GOETH FORTH FULL OF HOPE. WHEN THE DAY IS FAR SPENT HE RETURNETH, SMELLING OF STRONG DRINK, AND THE TRUTH IS NOT IN HIM.

"Behold the Fisherman!" Some 1911 angling humor.

Bluegills—over 2-1/2 pounds

Lake Trout—over 32 pounds

Rainbow Trout/Steelhead—over 14 pounds

Brown Trout—over 12 pounds

Brook Trout—over 5-1/2 pounds

Chinook (King) Salmon—over 20 pounds

Mud Catfish—over 55 pounds

Channel Catfish—over 30 pounds

Lake Sturgeon—over 140 pounds

Burbot (Eelpout)—over 12 pounds

Sheepshead—over 22 pounds

Carp—over 45 pounds

Remember that the fish must be from MINNESOTA waters. Be sure to include as much pertinent data as possible: catcher, where from, place caught, date, names and addresses of witnesses

237

and weigh-in officials, weights and measurements of the fish, press coverage, awards, etc.

Or you might know some special details about a catch in this Minnesota lunker list.

Send your information to:

CLASSIC MINNESOTA FISHING STORIES
Waldman House Press
525 North Third Street
Minneapolis, Minnesota 55401